BioCritiques

Maya Angelou
Jane Austen
The Brontë Sisters
Lord Byron
Geoffrey Chaucer
Anton Chekhov
Stephen Crane
Emily Dickinson
William Faulkner
F. Scott Fitzgerald
Robert Frost
Ernest Hemingway
Langston Hughes
Stephen King
Arthur Miller
Toni Morrison
Edgar Allan Poe
J. D. Salinger
William Shakespeare
John Steinbeck
Mark Twain
Alice Walker
Walt Whitman
Tennessee Williams

ROBERT FROST

Edited and with an introduction by
Harold Bloom
Sterling Professor of the Humanities
Yale University

CHELSEA HOUSE PUBLISHERS
Philadelphia

Printed and bound in the United States of America

10 9 8 7 6 5 4 3 2 1

Library of Congress Cataloging-in-Publication Data applied for

ISBN 0-7910-6183-3 (hc)

0-7910-7114-6 (pbk)

Chelsea House Publishers
1974 Sproul Road, Suite 400
Broomall, PA 19008-0914

http://www.chelseahouse.com

Contributing editor: Thomas March

Layout by EJB Publishing Services

CONTENTS

USER'S GUIDE

These volumes are designed to introduce the reader to the life and work of the world's literary masters. Each volume begins with Harold Bloom's essay "The Work in the Writer" and a volume-specific introduction also written by Professor Bloom. Following these unique introductions is an engaging biography that discusses the major life events and important literary accomplishments of the author under consideration.

Furthermore, each volume includes an original critique that not only traces the themes, symbols, and ideas apparent in the author's works, but strives to put those works into cultural and historical perspectives. In addition to the original critique is a brief selection of significant critical essays previously published on the author and his or her works followed by a concise and informative chronology of the writer's life. Finally, each volume concludes with a bibliography of the writer's works, a list of additional readings, and an index of important themes and ideas.

HAROLD BLOOM

The Work in the Writer

Literary biography found its masterpiece in James Boswell's *Life of Samuel Johnson*. Boswell, when he treated Johnson's writings, implicitly commented upon Johnson as found in his work, even as in the great critic's life. Modern instances of literary biography, such as Richard Ellmann's lives of W. B. Yeats, James Joyce, and Oscar Wilde, essentially follow in Boswell's pattern.

That the writer somehow is in the work, we need not doubt, though with William Shakespeare, writer-of-writers, we almost always need to rely upon pure surmise. The exquisite rancidities of the Problem Plays or Dark Comedies seem to express an extraordinary estrangement of Shakespeare from himself. When we read or attend *Troilus and Cressida* and *Measure for Measure*, we may be startled by particular speeches of Ulysses in the first play, or of Vincentio in the second. These speeches, of Ulysses upon hierarchy or upon time, or of Duke Vincentio upon death, are too strong either for their contexts or for the characters of their speakers. The same phenomenon occurs with Parolles, the military impostor of *All's Well That Ends Well*. Utterly disgraced, he nevertheless affirms: "Simply the thing I am/Shall make me live."

In Shakespeare, more even than in his peers, Dante and Cervantes, meaning always starts itself again through excess or overflow. The strongest of Shakespeare's creatures—Falstaff, Hamlet, Iago, Lear, Cleopatra—have an exuberance that is fiercer than their plays can contain. If Ben Jonson was at all correct in his complaint that "Shakespeare wanted art," it could have been only in a sense that he may not have intended. Where do the personalities of Falstaff or Hamlet touch a limit? What was it in Shakespeare that made the two parts of *Henry IV* and *Hamlet* into "plays unlimited"? Neither Falstaff nor Hamlet will be stopped: their wit, their beautiful, laughing speech, their intensity of being—all these are virtually infinite.

In what ways do Falstaff and Hamlet manifest the writer in the work? Evidently, we can never know, or know enough to answer with any authority. But what would happen if we reversed the question, and asked: How did the work form the writer, Shakespeare?

Of Shakespeare's inwardness, his biography tells us nothing. And yet, to an astonishing extent, Shakespeare created our inwardness. At the least, we can speculate that Shakespeare so lived his life as to conceal the depths of his nature, particularly as he rather prematurely aged. We do not have Shakespeare on Shakespeare, as any good reader of the Sonnets comes to realize: they do not constitute a key that unlocks his heart. No sequence of sonnets could be less confessional or more powerfully detached from the poet's self.

The German poet and universal genius, Goethe, affords a superb contrast to Shakespeare. Of Goethe's life, we know more than everything; I wonder sometimes if we know as much about Napoleon or Freud or any other human being who ever has lived, as we know about Goethe. Everywhere, we can find Goethe in his work, so much so that Goethe seems to crowd the writing out, just as Byron and Oscar Wilde seem to usurp their own literary accomplishments. Goethe, cunning beyond measure, nevertheless invested a rival exuberance in his greatest works that could match his personal charisma. The sublime outrageousness of the Second Part of *Faust*, or of the greater lyric and meditative poems, form a Counter-Sublime to Goethe's own daemonic intensity.

Goethe was fascinated by the daemonic in himself; we can doubt that Shakespeare had any such interests. Evidently, Shakespeare abandoned his acting career just before he composed *Measure for Measure* and *Othello*. I surmise that the egregious interventions by Vincentio and Iago displace the actor's energies into a new kind of mischief-making, a fresh opening to a subtler playwriting-within-the-play.

But what had opened Shakespeare to this new awareness? The answer is the work in the writer, *Hamlet* in Shakespeare. One can go further: it was not so much the play, *Hamlet*, as the character Hamlet, who changed Shakespeare's art forever.

Hamlet's personality is so large and varied that it rivals Goethe's own. Ironically Goethe's Faust, his Hamlet, has no personality at all, and is as colorless as Shakespeare himself seems to have chosen to be. Yet nothing could be more colorful than the Second Part of *Faust*, which is peopled by an astonishing array of monsters, grotesque devils, and classical ghosts.

A contrast between Shakespeare and Goethe demonstrates that in each—but in very different ways—we can better find the work in the person, than we can discover that banal entity, the person in the work. Goethe to many of his contemporaries, seemed to be a mortal god. Shakespeare, so far as we know, seemed an affable, rather ordinary fellow, who aged early and became somewhat withdrawn. Yet Faust, though Mephistopheles battles for his soul, is hardly worth the trouble unless you take him as an idea and not as a person. Hamlet is nearly every-idea-in-one, but he is precisely a personality and a person.

Would Hamlet be so astonishingly persuasive if his father's ghost did not haunt him? Falstaff is more alive than Prince Hal, who says that the devil haunts him in the shape of an old fat man. Three years before composing the final *Hamlet*, Shakespeare invented Falstaff, who then never ceased to haunt his creator. Falstaff and Hamlet may be said to best represent the work in the writer, because their influence upon Shakespeare was prodigious. W.H. Auden accurately observed that Falstaff possesses infinite energy: never tired, never bored, and absolutely both witty and happy until Hal's rejection destroys him. Hamlet too has infinite energy, but in him it is more curse than blessing.

Falstaff and Hamlet can be said to occupy the roles in Shakespeare's invented world that Sancho Panza and Don Quixote possess in Cervantes's. Shakespeare's plays from 1610 on (starting with *Twelfth Night*) are thus analogous to the Second Part of Cervantes's epic novel. Sancho and the Don overtly jostle Cervantes for authorship in the Second Part, even as Cervantes battles against the impostor who has pirated a continuation of his work. As a dramatist, Shakespeare manifests the work in the writer more indirectly. Falstaff's prose genius is revived in the scapegoating of Malvolio by Maria and Sir Toby Belch, while Falstaff's darker insights are developed by Feste's melancholic wit. Hamlet's intellectual resourcefulness, already deadly, becomes poisonous in Iago and in Edmund. Yet we have not crossed into the deeper abysses of the work in the writer in later Shakespeare.

No fictive character, before or since, is Falstaff's equal in self-trust. Sir John, whose delight in himself is contagious, has total confidence both in his self-awareness and in the resources of his language. Hamlet, whose self is as strong, and whose language is as copious, nevertheless distrusts both the self and language. Later Shakespeare is, as it were, much under the influence both of Falstaff and of Hamlet, but they tug him in opposite directions. Shakespeare's own copiousness of language is well-nigh incredible: a vocabulary in excess of twenty-one thousand words, almost eighteen hundred of which he coined himself. And of his word-hoard, nearly half are used only once each, as though the perfect setting for each had been found, and need not be repeated. Love for language and faith in language are Falstaffian attributes. Hamlet will darken both that love and that faith in Shakespeare, and perhaps the Sonnets can best be read as Falstaff and Hamlet counterpointing against one another.

Can we surmise how aware Shakespeare was of Falstaff and Hamlet, once they had played themselves into existence? *Henry IV, Part I* appeared in six quarto editions during Shakespeare's lifetime; *Hamlet* possibly had four. Falstaff and Hamlet were played again and again at the Globe, but Shakespeare knew also that they were being read, and he must have had contact with some of those readers. What would it have been like to discuss Falstaff or Hamlet with one of their early readers (presumably also part of their audience at the Globe), if you were the creator of such demiurges? The question would seem nonsensical to most Shakespeare scholars, but then these days they tend to be either ideologues or moldy figs. How can we recover the uncanniness of Falstaff and of Hamlet, when they now have become so familiar?

A writer's influence upon himself is an unexplored problem in criticism, but such an influence is never free from anxieties. The biocritical problem (which this series attempts to explore) can be divided into two areas, difficult to disengage fully. Accomplished works affect the author's life, and also affect her subsequent writings. It is simpler for me to surmise the effect of *Mrs. Dalloway* and *To the Lighthouse* upon Woolf's late *Between the Acts*, than it is to relate Clarissa Dalloway's suicide and Lily Briscoe's capable endurance in art to the tragic death and complex life of Virginia Woolf.

There are writers whose lives were so vivid that they seem sometimes to obscure the literary achievement: Byron, Wilde, Malraux, Hemingway. But most major Western writers do not live that exuberantly, and the greatest of all, Shakespeare, sometimes appears to have adopted the personal mask of colorlessness. And yet there are heroes of literature who struggled titanically with their own eras—Tolstoy, Milton, Victor Hugo—who nevertheless matter more for their works than their lives.

There are great figures—Emily Dickinson, Wallace Stevens, Willa Cather—who seem to have had so little of the full intensity of life when compared to the vitality of their work, that we might almost speak of the work in the work, rather than even of the work in a person. Emily Brontë might well be the extreme instance of such a visionary, surpassing William Blake in that one regard.

I conclude this general introduction to a series of literary bio-critiques by stating a tentative formula or principle for gauging the many ways in which the work influences the person and her subsequent, later work. Our influence upon ourselves is always related to the Shakespearean invention of self-overhearing, which I have written about in several other contexts. Life, as well as poetry and prose, is overheard rather than simply heard. The writer listens to herself as though she were somebody else, and the will to change begins to operate. The forces that live in us include the prior work we have done, and the dreams and waking visions that evade our dismissals.

HAROLD BLOOM

Introduction

Frost died two months short of his eighty-ninth birthday in 1963. That he was the major poet of 20th-century America can be both affirmed and disputed. But even the admirers of his strongest rivals—Wallace Stevens, T.S. Eliot, Hart Crane, Elizabeth Bishop—concede Frost's unique eminence as a poet both popular and sophisticated. There is a mountain in Ripton, Vermont, named after Robert Frost; no one is going to name a mountain after Wallace Stevens or Thomas Stearns Eliot.

Political correctness, rampant both in the media and in the universities, has given us a number of "popular poets" who are not poets at all. Frost, read by hundreds of thousands, is a great poet by all the aesthetic and cognitive standards that have been crucial to the Western Canon at least since Dante and Petrarch. I have just been sent a book of eighteen essays called *Harold Bloom's Shakespeare*. Fourteen of the essays contrive to be both abusive and unreadable. One denounces me as a "Patriarchal Eurocentric" another terms me "racist" for considering Caliban (son of a Berber witch and a sea-creature) to be something other than a heroic black freedom-fighter; several label me "sexist," and the nastiest devotes itself to an all-out attack upon my dust-jacket photograph as being "alarming and confrontational" (In merest actuality, I was shivering in a cold wind upon my porch, and plaintively was urging the photographer that it was time we went back inside).

Political correctness may prove permanent: New York City is about to be urged on a reading-bee, utilizing an adequate-enough book, chosen however for the ethnic origins of its author. After a third of a century fighting the decline and fall of our higher culture, I am aware that my side

1

has been defeated and routed: "They have the numbers, we have the heights." And yet the battlefield was ill-chosen: the British commonwealth nations, like the American elitist media and academics of once-higher education, were lost from the start. The authentic field for the struggle is across America, where the *New York Times* and Harvard hold no sway, and in much of Europe and the rest of the literate world. The lemmings of Resentment are ignored wherever women and men still love to read, questing for aesthetic sensation and cognitive enhancement. I know this from direct experience, each time I have gone out, here and abroad, on behalf of my books of the last decade or so.

Robert Frost's poetry, invulnerable to the tides of Resentment, becomes stronger with each passing year. Its values indeed are aesthetic and cognitive: it gives difficult pleasure, implicitly urging us to abandon easier pleasures, and it educates us up to Frost's own high standards. Frost himself, whom I met a few times, at Yale and at Breadloaf, was a difficult personality, at least in his old age. A superb monologist, he held one by his bursts of eloquence and his poetic authority. Some of the later poetry is self-indulgent, but always there are moments of vitalizing realization, as here in "Pod of the Milkweed," the opening poem in Frost's final volume, *In the Clearing* (1962):

> But waste was the essence of the scheme.
> And all the good they did for man or god
> To all those flowers they passionately trod
> Was leave as their posterity one pod
> With an inheritance of restless dream.

If a single pod is of the essence, the vision might seem minimalist, but Frost is too shrewd and too large for such ironic reductiveness, even when it is his own. Like Walt Whitman, with whom he has nothing else in common, he was an Emersonian. Frost placed Emerson's "Uriel" first among Western poems. That is sublime overpraise, but reading "Uriel" now, one uncannily hears the poetic voice of Robert Frost:

> Line in nature is not found;
> Unit and universe are round;
> In vain produced, all rays return;
> Evil will bless, and ice will burn.

Frost's voice, at its strongest, can be found in a plethora of his poems: "A Servant to Servants," "The Wood-Pile," "The Oven Bird," "Putting in the Seed," "Two Watches," "Once by the Pacific," "The Flower Bust," "Two

Tramps in Mud Time," "Design," "Provide, Provide," "The Most of It,"
"Never Again Would Birds' Song Be the Same," "The Subverted Flower,"
"A Cabin in the Clearing." That is a personal list of fourteen; the fifteenth
and best seems to me "Directive," for it has the whole of Frost in it.

"Directive" is the fourth poem in the later volume, *Steeple Bush* (1947).
It is a retrospective vision of his life by a man of seventy-three, and is
animated by an astonishing harshness, both towards the poet and the reader.
Opening with a powerfully monosyllabic line—"Back out of all this now too
much for us"—Frost takes his reader and himself on a journey to the interior,
past and inward:

> Back in a time made simple by the loss
> Of detail, burned, dissolved, and broken off
> Like graveyard marble sculpture in the weather.

We go back to a house, farm, town all now obliterated by time, and we
take a road that is more like a quarry. The going back is a "serial ordeal," an
Arthurian testing to see if we are worthy to quest for the Holy Grail, a quest
wholly ironized in "Directive":

> Your destination and your destiny's
> A brook that was the water of the house,
> *   *   *   *   *
>
> I have kept hidden in the instep arch
> Of an old cedar at the waterside
> A broken drinking goblet like the Grail
> Under a spell so the wrong ones can't find it,
> So can't get saved, as Saint Mark says they mustn't.

The Gospel of Mark (4:11–12) gives us, just this once, a Jesus incredibly
harsh:

> That seeing they may see, and not perceive, and hearing they
> may hear, and not understand, lest at any time, they should be
> converted, and their sins should be forgiven them.

But if we *are* among Frost's elect, to be saved by the poet, then:

> Here are your waters and your watering place.
> Drink and be whole again beyond confusion.

The poem is only a "momentary stay against confusion," Frost had said elsewhere. With a desperate irony, he hopes for something more, for himself and for us, here at the conclusion of "Directive."

BRUCE AND BECKY DUROST FISH

Biography of Robert Frost

A MAN OF CONTRADICTIONS

The winter sun glared down on the crowd gathered that bitterly cold morning of January 20, 1961. A lean, stooped man with a shock of white hair walked slowly to the outdoor podium. The 86-year-old poet was one of the few men present who wore no hat. His simple black overcoat whipped in the winter wind, providing little protection from the stinging cold. In the crowd around him and across the country, millions of eyes followed Robert Frost's every move as he fumbled with the pages of a manuscript and squinted down at the words. The strong light deepened the age lines across his pale forehead and down the sides of his angular face. Contrasting shadows brought out the unhealthy hollowness of his cheeks. He appeared too frail to stand, much less to read anything.

At long last, in a halting voice he began to speak the words of a poem he had composed for this important national event. He had still been working on the piece, "For John F. Kennedy: His Inauguration," earlier that morning and had not had time to memorize it—something he usually did before reciting poetry in public. Fresh gusts of wind ripped at the pages in his hands, turning the words before him to unintelligible blurs. Even when he steadied the paper, the words remained vague. His aging eyes could no longer adjust to the harsh daylight.

Suddenly he stopped. "I'm not having a good light here at all," he muttered. "I can't see in this light." [Meyers, 323] The microphone picked up his whispered words and amplified them clearly to the farthest edge of the crowd. People applauded warmly, seeming to want to encourage their favorite poet. Newly sworn in Vice President Lyndon B. Johnson got up from his seat among the dignitaries and crossed the platform to assist Frost. Johnson pulled off his silk top hat and used it to create a shadow. His efforts didn't help. The shadow was too dark, and the words became invisible.

"Here, let me help you," Frost said as he grabbed the hat from the vice president. [Meyers, 323] The crowd laughed and applauded. Suddenly the old poet gained new life. He waved the vice president aside, grabbed the fistful of pages from the podium, and held them up to the crowd, explaining that the pages held the preface to a poem he did not have to read.

Straightening, he began instead to recite a different poem, one that had long been a part of his soul and whose words he spoke with authority and conviction:

> The land was ours before we were the land's.
> She was our land more than a hundred years
> Before we were her people. . . . [Parini, 335]

The crowd huddled in front of the nation's capitol listened in rapt silence. More than 60 million Americans sitting in front of their black-and-white television sets joined them. As the poet continued to speak, millions claimed his words as their own. When he reached the last line of "The Gift Outright," Robert Frost slowed the pace, adding emphasis to certain words: "Such as she was, such as she *would* become, *has* become, and I—and for this occasion let me change that to—what she *will* become." [Parini, 414] The crowd burst into cheers as he quietly returned to his seat.

The next morning, the *Washington Post* declared, "Robert Frost in his natural way stole the hearts of the Inaugural crowd." [Parini, 415] But that verdict was surprising news to Frost. "I came through that almost miraculously," he later explained. "I went home thinking I'd made a mess of it, very depressed . . . I was feeling kind of sick at heart. Then everybody began to say I did wonders. Some said, 'I bet you did all that on purpose,' it was a show I put on. I hadn't thought of that. The wind and the sun and the cold—I just couldn't read, that's all—nothing was right." [Meyers, 323]

Robert Frost might easily have expressed those same sentiments in summing up his entire life. For decades, the man who became America's best-loved poet was tormented by the conflict between the success of his work and his own self-doubts. The foundation for that continuing turmoil was laid early in life, as Robert Frost, the quintessential New England poet, was growing up—in California.

A Tumultuous Childhood

From the moment he was born on March 26, 1874, Robert Lee Frost was immersed in a chaotic environment with conflicting messages. Even the choice of his name was emotionally charged. His father, William Frost Jr., although descending from an old New England family chose to name his son after the southern Civil War hero Robert E. Lee.

The name choice was an emphatic but typical rejection of William Frost's northern roots. A brilliant, driven man, he used his gifts to rebel against almost everything his Massachusetts family stood for. As a teenager, he ran away from home to join the Confederate Army. He got as far as Philadelphia before he was caught by police and returned to his angry parents. After graduating from Harvard University in 1872 with honors (and a reputation for partying), the elder Frost rejected a job offer from the mill where his own father was foreman and became instead the principal of a private school in Lewistown, Pennsylvania.

The young man viewed this job as a necessary step in his plan to reach San Francisco and build a career in journalism and politics. The position also got him away from his parents and their strict lifestyle. What he did not foresee was the affect Belle Moodie, a teacher at the academy six years older than he, would have on him. Belle was born near Edinburgh, Scotland. Three years after her father drowned at sea when she was eight, Belle was shipped by her mother to Ohio to live with a wealthy aunt and uncle.

William and Belle had obvious differences. He was impetuous and rebellious with little use for organized religion, preferring instead a rationalistic approach to life's questions. She was demure and cautious, drawn to the mystical and non-rational aspects of religion and life. But the two shared a love of literature and ideas. Within five months, Frost proposed; Belle turned him down; he persisted, and they married at the end of the school year. They then resigned from their jobs, and traveled to the Ohio home of Belle's aunt and uncle, where she stayed while her husband went to San Francisco to make arrangements for their new life. Frost found employment at the *San Francisco Bulletin* and the young couple soon settled into their first home. Young Robert was born a year later. The joyous event was not free from conflict. Family legend says that William threatened to shoot the doctor if anything went wrong with his son's birth.

William Frost enjoyed his young family, but the task of parenting took its toll on both parents and the young father began spending evenings in the local pub gambling usually losing.

Belle Frost hated housekeeping and cooking so after a year in a rented house, the family moved to a hotel, which provided housekeeping services and a chance for socializing. For the rest of their married lives, Belle and William Frost moved frequently, alternating between rented homes and hotel suites.

But Belle missed the companionship of her husband. As he spent more time in pubs, she became more involved in the Swedenborgian Church. This small group followed the teachings of 18th-century philosopher Emanuel Swedenborg, who believed he could communicate with spirits and angels. His mystical and intellectually stimulating teachings provided an escape from the dissatisfaction Belle felt toward life.

Belle could not completely ignore her circumstances, however. Her husband's drinking caused him to become more violent toward his family. In 1876, pregnant with her second child, Belle took Robert and left. Traveling by train and coach, she crossed the country and arrived in Lawrence, Massachusetts, where her in-laws lived. The elder Frosts were not happy to see their daughter-in-law but let Belle and Robert stay.

On June 25, 1876, Jeanie Florence Frost was born. Two-year-old Robert had a little sister. The Frost grandparents made it clear that they hated having young children underfoot, so soon after delivering her baby girl, Belle and her children left to visit one of her college friends for several weeks.

Although separated, the Frosts corresponded and were able to resolve some of their differences. When William, who loved sports, became ill after running in a six-day race, Belle worried that he wasn't taking care of himself. Returning in September to San Francisco she stopped briefly in Ohio meeting up with an old high school friend, Blanche Rankin, who decided to travel with them to San Francisco. Blanche planned to live temporarily with the Frosts while she found a teaching job but became instead a fixture in their household for the next eight years.

Belle's worst fears about her husband were realized when she reached San Francisco and found him in a hospital thinner, jaundiced, and coughing blood. William denied the seriousness of his illness and, once he was released from the hospital, took whiskey to cure his ailments. With similar poor judgment he invested his extra cash into silver mines, a high-risk and usually losing proposition.

In the midst of such turmoil, Robert and little sister Jeanie were well cared for by their mother and "Aunt" Blanche. Both women had been teachers and emphasized discipline and traditional education. They entered Robert in both kindergarten and first grade, but after he complained of stomach pains, they brought him home and taught him there. Belle often read to her two children and made sure that they knew about Scotland's heroes and poets.

William's drinking problems did not compensate for his charm. Increasingly, he became belligerent and home life was marked by violence. The family made every effort to avoid upsetting the sick, unpredictable man, but was not always successful. One time, a drunken Frost flew into a rage at the mess made by his son and a friend who were building a model ship with scraps of wood and glue on the living-room floor. He grabbed his son and struck him with the back of his hand several times. In response to these episodes Belle and Blanche sometimes indulged the little boy. When William Frost was sober, he often took his son on walks through the city, introducing him to the wide variety of people he met as a reporter. The family often went to the beach for picnics sponsored by a Scottish society Belle belonged to. The adults danced to Celtic music played by fiddlers, while the children ran races. William Frost took great pride in his son's sprinting ability and once bought him a special pair of running shoes.

As it turned out, Robert's sprinting talent came in handy when he was playing on the San Francisco streets. In the 1870s, the city was full of rough characters and many homeless boys were doing whatever was necessary to survive. Robert befriended some of these boys, in part because he was free to spend the afternoons as he liked. One time he and his new friends stole a pig and sold it to a Chinese merchant. They also had frequent fistfights. Robert later boasted about his abilities:

> [I said] I could lick any two boys the size of one I named. The kids went out and brought in two boys. They didn't wait for me to jump 'em, but they jumped me first. I grabbed one around the neck and tried to gouge his eyes out. The other danced round and round and when he had a chance would rush in and scratch me. I was pretty well all in when we were separated, and I had to be taken home. Apparently nobody won the fight. My mother sent for a doctor who fixed up my scratches and gouged eyes. [Meyers, 11]

Frost's mother was appalled at these activities, but his father saw them as a sign that his son would stand up for himself.

Even with his poor health, William Frost loved political action. An avid Democrat, he worked on three presidential campaigns and was a delegate to the 1880 Democratic National Convention. The Democrats lost the first two presidential campaigns, but in 1884 William backed the victorious Grover Cleveland. That same year 10-year-old son Robert saw his father run for city tax collector. William lost and went on a drinking binge for several days.

Such behavior diminished William's already slim chance of recovery from what had been diagnosed as tuberculosis. In desperation, he tried, in vain, a number of folk remedies—including a visit to a slaughterhouse with, young Robert in tow, to drink the blood of a freshly slaughtered steer.

By the spring of 1885, William was too weak to leave home and was coughing up blood regularly. He often asked his young son to lie beside him on the sofa for added warmth, but in the process he exposed him to tuberculosis. In the middle of April, 34-year-old William Frost wrote to his parents in Massachusetts, telling them of his impending death and asking for financial help. "You must do what you can for [my family]," he wrote. [Parini, 18]

On May 5, the children were sent outside to play. A short while later, another child told them, "There's crepe on your door." [Meyers, 13] Crepe was a sign of death in a family and in this way the young Frost children learned that their father was gone.

Life changed quickly. The $20,000 life insurance benefit for Belle had been lost through William's, and after paying her bills she was left with only eight dollars. Belle's in-laws sent money to ship their son's body back to Massachusetts for burial and to pay the traveling expenses for Belle and the two children. The young widow disliked her in-laws, but she needed their support in order to start a new life. She packed their possessions and with the children boarded a train for the journey east. Eleven-year-old Robert later told a friend that it was "the *longest, loneliest* train ride he ever took." [Parini, 19]

Life felt even lonelier when he arrived in Massachusetts. Years later, here called, "At first I disliked the Yankees. They were cold. They seemed narrow to me. I could not get used to them." [Thompson, 48] After a brief stay with relatives, the three Frosts moved to Salem, New Hampshire, where Belle Frost taught in a small school, earning just nine dollars a week. Young Frost helped out by taking part-time jobs. He recalled:

> One year when I was twelve I worked in a shoe shop, inserting nails into holes in the heels of shoes. I held the nails in my mouth (Mother did not realize that) but I never inhaled or swallowed any. Then next year, I was thirteen, I worked behind a big machine run by a big man—that process was really dangerous for a child but I didn't let her know or lose a finger. [Sergeant, 19]

The job was dangerous but also boring. He couldn't quit without his mother's permission, so he told her that the men swore and she immediately let him leave. Getting out of work seemed to be one of young Robert's favorite activities in his early teen years. In school, he often asked to be excused to use the outhouse, and he hid his whittling activity behind the large geography book on his desk he was supposed to be reading

Family life continued to be difficult. Belle was losing control over her son and her own classroom as a result of a debilitating illness that also dramatically changed her appearance. Her status as a teacher became controversial and uncertain. Students commented on her sloppy appearance while her defenders praised her for getting four students accepted by the local high school, a academic feat regarded by the community as exceptional.

That summer, Frost was introduced to Jane Porter's novel *The Scottish Chiefs*. He was so captivated by the conflicts it portrayed that he read the book straight through. He later said that it was the first book he read completely. It would not be his last. From that moment, Robert Lee Frost became a different student. He passed the admissions test for the high school in Lawrence with impressive scores and quickly worked his way to the head of his class.

Frost was a loner in high school, awkward in his ill-fitting clothes and insecure socially because of the family's precarious financial position. In his sophomore year, he befriended Carl Burell—an older student in his mid-twenties—who had returned to school after 10 years of supporting himself by doing odd jobs. Carl loved books, and the two students spent hours discussing science and philosophical ideas.

In the summer of 1890, following Frost's sophomore year, the family's desperate finances necessitated a move to a hotel in Ocean Park, Maine, where Belle and Jeanie worked as chambermaids, and Robert did odd jobs.

That fall, the Frosts returned to Massachusetts. Belle had a teaching job in Methuen, and the children entered their third year at Lawrence High School. In preparation for the preliminary entrance exams for Harvard University, Frost spent hours translating Cicero, Virgil, and Ovid from Latin into English.

In the fall of 1891, Frost was on top of his world: high school senior; editor of the school newspaper; and competing for the honor of being named class valedictorian. In October, he performed well on a second set of exams for Harvard. He was concerned, though, about the health of his sister, Jeanie, who was showing classic symptoms of what is now called bipolar mood disorder. Sometimes she flew into rages and seemed out of control. Other times she sulked and refused to see any of her friends. In December of Frost's senior year, Jeanie was hospitalized for typhoid fever and dropped out of school permanently.

Frost also suffered from depression; perhaps for fear of becoming like his sister, he threw himself into academic and athletic activities. His efforts were rewarded. On a hot, muggy Thursday near the end of June, 1892, Lawrence High School graduated 32 seniors. The last of 13 student speakers, Frost became terrified and almost bolted from the room. Resisting that impulse, he successfully delivered his address. The next day, a local newspaper stated that Frost's speech "combined in a rare degree poetic thought, a fine range of imagination, and devotion to a high ideal, and evinced intellectual compass much beyond the usual school essay." [Parini, 31]

As proud as Frost was of his academic accomplishments, he was even more pleased by his relationship with Elinor White, his rival for class valedictorian. They became secretly engaged that summer. He pushed for getting married immediately, but she wanted to wait until they had both completed their college educations. Her parents were sending her to St. Lawrence University in Canton, New York Frost's plans to attend Harvard were short-circuited when his grandfather complained that it was a "drinking" school and reminded Belle of the wild life her husband had fallen into while a student there. Instead, Frost entered Dartmouth College in Hanover, New Hampshire, with dreams of achieving academic success and the reward of marriage to Elinor.

THE SHAPING OF A POET

Frost's dreams of college life clashed rudely with reality. Dartmouth was then an all-male college with a long tradition of sophomores hazing freshmen. With his experiences with street boys in San Francisco and the rougher individuals at the mills where he had worked, Frost was prepared to deal with the often harsh features of hazing. He even enjoyed some of Dartmouth's traditions, including a version of Capture the Flag in which freshmen attempted to steal the sophomore pennant. Frost's athletic abilities contributed to the success of his class in the game.

Frost also wanted to study, but hazing made it impossible to work in his room, which he shared with the only other freshman in the building. The two boys were often awakened by sophomores in the middle of the night, and no matter how they barricaded their door, the other students successfully broke in. To avoid victimization, Frost fell into the habit of taking long walks at night. Dartmouth was located in a remote area of New Hampshire, and the young student hiked in the wooded mountains. Other students viewed these nighttime sojourns with suspicion and asked him what he was doing. His answer bewildered them: "I gnaw bark." [Parini, 35]

Despite his intellectual enthusiasm, Frost found his classes boring. Many students seemed satisfied to memorize material for tests rather than ask questions or think independently. To him, college seemed to be "conducted with the almost express purpose of keeping [a student] busy with something else till the danger of his ever creating anything is passed." [Meyers, 23]

The frustrated student did manage to write some poems and sent lengthy letters to Elinor. He was concerned that, rather than becoming miserable because of his absence, she was enjoying college life.

By Thanksgiving, Frost's fears about Elinor, frustrations with classes, and letters from home describing his mother's struggle to control her students combined to make him discouraged. He and a friend took part in a haircutting prank in which another boy's hair was cut in a strange fashion that formed a "picture" on the back of his head. Many sources agree that this prank led to Robert Frost being expelled from Dartmouth because administrators wanted to set an example and end the extremes of hazing. Frost always said he had left Dartmouth of his own will, but he also was known for deliberately misleading biographers.

Whether willingly or not, Frost left Dartmouth before he had completed his first semester. He returned to Lawrence to face general disapproval from family and neighbors. They thought he had thrown away an opportunity to get a good education and become part of a well-paying profession.

In the next two years, he drifted from one job to another. He taught school, worked in factories, and wrote for newspapers. The Methuen school district fired his mother, concluding that she was incapable of controlling her students. Frost became responsible for the financial security of his family.

Although neighbors suspected that Frost would never amount to anything, he quietly put himself on a strict program of self-improvement. "To love poetry is to study it," he maintained, and study it he did. [Parini, 44] He learned Greek in order to read works by Homer in their original language, and he spent hours engrossed in Shakespeare and the English poets Keats, Shelley, Tennyson, and Browning.

This work had an effect on his poetry. In 1894, he composed "My Butterfly," which he called his "first real poem." In a story he recounted many times, he said he had written it "all in one go in the kitchen of our house on Tremont Street. I locked the door and all the time I was working, Jeanie my sister tried to batter it down and get in." [Parini, 42]

Jeanie's mental deterioration increased the instability of the Frost household. Frost found writing poetry to be "a momentary stay against confusion." As he wrote "My Butterfly," he experienced a sense that "something was happening. It was like cutting along a nerve." [Parini, 42]

The result was a poem many critics consider to contain the first indications of Frost's unique voice. These lines are from the second stanza:

> The gray grass is scarce dappled with the snow;
> Its two banks have not shut upon the river;
> But it is long ago—
> It seems forever—
> Since first I saw thee glance,
> With all thy dazzling other ones,
> In airy dalliance,
> Precipitate in love,
> Tossed, tangled, whirled and whirled above,
> Like a limp rose-wreath in a fairy dance. [Parini, 43]

Pleased with his work, Frost submitted "My Butterfly" to *The Independent*, a respected national journal edited by William Hayes. It was his first published poem. Susan Hayes Ward, William Hayes' sister and managing editor of *The Independent*, began writing to Frost about the technical aspects of poetry; their correspondence would continue for more than 20 years.

The Wards put the young poet into contact with influential people interested in helping writers. One of these, William E. Wolcott, a minister from Lawrence, having read a selection of Frost's unpublished poems, suggested that the poet "elevate" the tone of his work because it sounded too much like the spoken voice. The 20-year-old poet vehemently disagreed with Wolcott's suggestions and became more determined to ground his work in the sounds of ordinary speech.

Frost also rejected another offer of help—this one from his grandfather. Recognizing that his grandson was a published poet, the elder Frost offered financial support for a year. If Frost did not become a successful poet by the end of that year, he would agree to give up his writing. Frost rejected the offer, arguing that it would take 20 years to become a recognized poet.

Struggling to sustain his family and live with the untreated mental illness of his sister and the stigma of being viewed as a failure by most of his acquaintances, Frost was again beset with depression. He feared that Elinor was enjoying the attentions of other young men at college. She still refused to marry him until she'd earned her degree. In desperation, Frost had two copies of some of his poems printed on handmade paper and bound in leather. One copy was to be his and the other hers. He took the train and paid an unexpected visit on Elinor at her school. She did not seem to appreciate the romantic gesture, and Frost left in complete despair, destroying his own copy of the poems during the trip home.

In November 1894, shortly after this disturbing visit, Frost received a letter from Elinor convincing him that their engagement was broken. He surreptitiously packed a bag and headed for the Dismal Swamp, which runs along the border between Virginia and North Carolina. Frost wanted to lose himself in a world that matched his mood. Other poets such as Longfellow, with whom he was familiar, used the Dismal Swamp in their writing as a place for those who have lost hope. Dark and cold, the swamp was full of bogs and quicksand. A tangle of briars and honeysuckle concealed water moccasins and rattlesnakes. Frost reportedly plunged into the morass, walking 10 miles before night fell.

As terrible as he felt, the young poet was not able to give up on life. He joined a group of duck hunters and made his way back to civilization. After several weeks of various misadventures, he wired his mother for the train fare back to Lawrence.

Everyone had worried about him, but wisely they did not make too much of his disappearance. He was determined to find steady employment and prove his worth to Elinor. He worked briefly at two newspapers, but in March 1985, he quit in disgust, just before Elinor came home for a visit. During a meeting at her family's home, Frost claimed that Elinor no longer believed in him and was responsible for his failures. She told him that if he felt that way, he could take his ring back. He grabbed the ring, threw it into the coal-burning kitchen stove, and stomped out of the house. Elinor rescued the ring from the fire and later the couple made up.

That spring, Frost and his mother started a private school with a few students. Even Jeanie helped out when her health allowed it. Elinor agreed to join them after her graduation from St. Lawrence in June.

On December 19, 1895, Frost and Elinor married. Elinor's father objected to the marriage and refused to pay for a church wedding. He thought Frost incurably lazy, unstable, and prone to temper tantrums and moodiness, but Elinor's mother encouraged the young couple. The wedding took place at the private school.

The Frosts almost immediately returned to teaching, delaying their honeymoon until summer. They could not afford a house, so they moved in with Frost's mother—a difficult situation for everyone. In March, Elinor discovered she was pregnant. Everyone was relieved that summer when the newlyweds were able to rent an inexpensive cottage in New Hampshire for a honeymoon. Returning to Lawrence, they moved into a separate apartment in a home Frost's mother had rented, giving them more privacy. On September 25, the Frost's first child, a boy, was born. Elinor, who had been somewhat depressed during her pregnancy, was thrilled with little Elliott.

Finances, however, remained a problem. By the winter of 1896, a desperate Frost applied for admission to Harvard, hoping that more education would earn him a better income. He was accepted for the fall 1897 term, and his grandfather once again funded his studies. There was no time to move his family to Cambridge that fall, but by winter, Elinor and Elliot along with Mrs. White, Elinor's mother, arrived, and the four moved into a small apartment. At the end of the semester, Frost received a $200 scholarship in recognition of his academic excellence. The scholarship confirmed his abilities, and eased the family's tight financial situation.

When Elinor became pregnant again, they decided that she and Elliot should stay with her parents while he returned to Cambridge in the fall of 1898. Although he continued to do well, he knew he would not complete his studies. "They could not make a student of me here, but they gave it their best," he later told a group of Harvard students. [Parini, 64] By March 1899, Frost was complaining of stomach and heart ailments and what he termed "nervous exhaustion," which was probably depression. The next month he left Harvard.

A doctor in Lawrence urged Frost to follow a more active life and recommended farming. With a loan from his grandfather, Frost rented a small farm near Methuen, and in June of that year was raising chickens and selling eggs. Lesley, who had arrived on April 28, moved with them to the farm.

Frost loved life on the farm, although it did hold challenges. His mother came to live with them after doctors told her that she had advanced cancer and would live less than a year. Frost's health improved, and his mother's cancer seemed to go into remission. In the first half of 1900, however, Elliott became quite ill. Elinor's mother, a Christian Scientist, argued against consulting a doctor; Frost, while not agreeing with his mother-in-law, put off taking action until early July, when Elliott developed chronic vomiting. Frost's own doctor arrived to announce, "It's too late now. The child will be dead by morning." [Parini, 68] The shocked parents stayed by Elliott's bedside all night, and at 4:00 A.M. on July 8, the boy died. Elinor became severely depressed, and Frost blamed himself for not calling his doctor sooner.

The situation did not improve. Elinor went into a severe decline and had to be moved to a sanitarium, Jeanie charged her brother with turning their mother out because she had become a burden. The Frosts' landlady stopped by to collect some back rent, and when she saw the unwashed dishes, dirty floors, and chickens, she gave them until the end of the month to leave.

Elinor's mother heard that a farm in Derry, New Hampshire, about 12 miles from Lawrence, was for sale for $1,700. After making sure that the property was in good condition and that the asking price was reasonable, Frost's grandfather agreed to buy the farm for them on condition that Frost let his high school friend Carl Burell work with him. The Frost family moved to the farm at the beginning of October.

Over the next 11 years, Frost found mixed success in farming, but that world and the people who filled it would shape his poetry. "It all started in Derry," he commented later, "the whole thing." [Parini, 72] Many of the poems in his first two published collections were initially written during those years. Frost was experiencing some of the life struggles that he later wrestled with in his poetry. Shortly after the move to Derry, his mother died of cancer. He entered another period of intense depression that only lifted with the arrival of spring. Then, in July of 1901, Frost's grandfather died.

Frost had often questioned his grandfather's love, but the old man remembered him in his will. He granted free use of the farm for 10 years, at which point his grandson could take possession. The elder Frost also left an annuity of $500 a year, increasing to $800 a year after 10 years. While Frost wouldn't be rich, the money would allow his family to live comfortably if they maintained a simple lifestyle.

Frost continued farming but didn't appreciate Carl Burell's continued presence. In 1902, he asked Burell to leave, soon discovered how difficult it could be to milk cows, and scandalized his rural neighbors by waiting until late morning to feed the animals.

The family continued to grow. On May 22, 1902, another son, whom they named Carol, was born. On June 27, 1902, Irma was born, and Marjorie followed on March 29, 1905. The Frosts decided to educate their children at home. The children also enjoyed tramping in the woods with their father, who would regale them with stories taken from history and great works of literature.

With a growing family and Frost's lack of skill in managing money, the family needed more income than they could get from the farm and annuity; so Frost took a position teaching at the Pinkerton Academy, located two miles from the farm. He was a popular, if unorthodox, teacher, and he threw himself into as many school activities as possible. In the spring of 1907, however, overwork led to a severe pneumonia from which Frost's doctor feared he would not recover. Frost stayed at home for two months, and Elinor, who was pregnant, became seriously ill herself. The Frosts' daughter Elinor Bettina was born on June 18 but died soon afterward.

In part because of their health problems, the Frosts decided to rent a home in Derry. Frost continued his highly successful career at Pinkerton until 1910, when he resigned. The suicide of their landlord in Derry greatly disturbed both parents, who worried about Carol's reaction to the death. In fact, Carol became obsessed with the idea of suicide.

In 1911, under the terms of his grandfather's will, Frost was free to sell the Derry farm. Unfortunately, he had paid little attention to maintaining the property once he had begun teaching, so he could not find a buyer. In the end he sold the mortgage to a bank for $1200, significantly less than the market value.

Frost also taught in Plymouth, New Hampshire, in 1911, but he soon reached a crossroads. He had to decide whether to pour his energies into teaching or writing poetry. In the spring of 1912, a number of magazines accepted Frost's poems for publication, so he decided to write. Money from the sale of the farm and the increased annuity enabled the Frosts to travel to either Canada or England for a year. Based on the flip of a coin, England won. Few people noticed when Frost, Elinor, and their four children left Boston aboard the SS *Parisian* on August 23, 1912. It would be one of the last trips Robert Frost made in obscurity.

THE ENGLISH YEARS

The voyage from Boston to Glasgow, Scotland, took a little over a week. Landing on the morning of September 2, 1912, the family traveled across Scotland and England, arriving at London that evening. They secured rooms at the Premier Hotel and felt, as Elinor stated in a letter to a friend, "greatly excited, you may imagine, at being all alone, without a single friend, in the biggest city in the world." [Parini, 116]

Energized by being in a new place, the Frosts were not about to end their day by unpacking. After putting the youngest children to bed and leaving 13-year-old Lesley in charge, the couple set out on a 10-minute walk to the Kingsway Theatre to take in George Bernard Shaw's drama *Fanny's First Play*, a witty attack on middle-class values.

While Elinor and the children enjoyed a variety of sightseeing tours, Frost searched frantically for housing. They could not afford to stay at the hotel indefinitely, and because the decision to travel to England had been made so quickly Frost had been unable to make other arrangements. He quickly discovered that rentals near London were quite expensive and eventually settled on a bungalow in Beaconsfield, about 40 minutes by train from London.

The home had two bedrooms, a living room, dining room, kitchen, cramped bathroom, and a low attic for storage space. The dining room would have to be converted into a bedroom, but the rent—$20 a month with a one-year lease—was quite reasonable. By the middle of September, the family had moved to their new home, and Frost arranged for their belongings that had been stored at the train station to be delivered. When the boxes arrived, he quickly reassembled Elinor's rocking chair and his favorite Morris chair with an adjustable back and broad arms—his favorite place for writing poetry. The family also purchased furniture for $125, more than they would spend on a year's rent. They planned on reselling the furniture before they returned to America.

The Frosts strongly disapproved of the local free school and refused to send their children to it, but they could not afford private school for four children. After much discussion, they decided to send their two oldest daughters, Lesley and Irma, to a nearby private school for girls and to have Elinor teach Marjorie and Carol at home. Frost helped by taking over some of the meal preparations—a job Elinor intensely disliked.

Frost wrote throughout the morning and into the afternoon. He made a futile attempt to write a novel but spent most of his time compiling poems for his first book of poetry, *A Boy's Will*. Like other poets, Frost struggled to arrange poems written over a period of years into some semblance of order and thematic continuity. Frost biographer Jay Parini has pointed out that Frost generally succeeded in his efforts:

> The lyrics of *A Boy's Will* do, however, play together rather well, tonally and stylistically. The poet-speaker generally assumes an implied listener, which lends a dramatic quality to their presentation. One can usually hear a dialectic at work as the poet-speaker attempts to reconcile his various moods, whether hopeful (as in "A Late Walk") or, more often, despairing (as in "Storm Fear"). [Parini, 120]

Elinor helped to arrange the poems and encouraged her husband to approach a publishing house. Daughter Lesley typed the hand-written poems and with the completed manuscript, probably in October, Frost traveled to London to find a publisher. In a 1921 newspaper interview, he described the trip:

> I went down to London to see a man whom I hardly knew. . . . I asked him if he knew of some small respectable publisher who might buy my poems and not kick me out of the door. He said that no one published poems and that I would myself have to pay to have them printed. I never wanted to do that. Somehow I never liked the idea.
>
> In the conversation this man named David Nutt. Then and there I went over to Nutt's establishment [and] left the poems . . . [Walsh, 36]

David Nutt's small firm was known among poets. It published many of the most popular British poets of the early 20th century, including John Drinkwater. Frost delivered his manuscript to Mrs. Nutt, who had inherited the business from her late husband. Her first impression on Frost was not good:

> I must admit that she eyed me suspiciously when I mentioned that I wanted a book of poetry published; she had a right to. And she was formidably enough dressed in her black outfit to have scared most anybody, almost scared me. . . . Then, having as she thought, disarmed me, she said she *might*, she just barely might publish it if I would pay part of the costs. I told her emphatically *no*. I would never do it. So I started to gather up my manuscript, which till then she had scarcely even glanced at, very firmly telling her I had never stooped to paying to have my poems published, and I would never do it. Seeing I was firm she softened a bit and told me to leave the manuscript and let her have a look at the poems. . . . After receiving her assurance that she would make her decision soon and notify me at Beaconsfield, I took the train back home very doubtful of the outcome. [Walsh, 40]

Near the end of October, Robert Frost received a card dated October 26, 1912. Scrawled in almost illegible handwriting was a note from Mrs. Nutt, accepting the manuscript but not offering terms for the contract. After weeks of silence, a meeting in London, and private consideration of the offered contract, Frost agreed to sell all rights to his poetry for 12 percent royalties, which would be payable only after the first 250 copies had sold. The first printing of *A Boy's Will* would run 1,000 copies. The poet also agreed to give Mrs. Nutt the first option on his next four books at the same terms, an arrangement that placed him at a significant disadvantage because the amount of money he earned from his books would not increase until he published a sixth volume of poetry.

In spite of the one-sidedness of the agreement, Frost was ecstatic about being published. Because the book was so small, the publisher scheduled printed copies to be on bookstore shelves by the end of February 1913.

In the fall of 1912, Robert Frost entered the most productive, sustained period of composition in his life. Both he and Elinor were amazed as day after day he began work early in the morning and often continued until late in the night. By spring, about a dozen finished poems lay on his desk, including "Mending Wall," "Home Burial," "After Apple-Picking," and "Birches," among the best-known poems in American literature.

His confidence buoyed by the scheduled release of his first book and his sudden upturn in productivity, Frost decided to test the London literary waters by attending the January 8, 1913, opening of the Poetry Bookshop. More than 300 people, including writers, artists, critics, book editors, and their fans, attended the event. That day, Frost met the English poet Frank (F.S.) Flint, who asked whether he had met Ezra Pound, another American writer living in England. When Frost answered no, Flint volunteered to arrange a meeting. He also offered to review Frost's book of poetry as soon as it was released.

As a result of Flint's efforts, Ezra Pound wrote a brief note to Frost, inviting him to visit at his home in the Kensington section of London. A decade younger than Frost, Pound already had a sizeable collection of work in print, including six volumes of poetry. It took Frost about two months to build up the courage to visit the well-known poet. In early March, Robert Frost made his pilgrimage to Kensington and knocked on the heavy oak door to Pound's flat. When the door opened, Frost saw a young man with bright red hair and beard, wearing a blue-and-green silk dressing gown. After telling Frost he was rude not have responded to his invitation sooner, Pound eagerly asked to see Frost's book. Frost replied that he had not yet received a copy. Pound threw on some clothes and insisted that they immediately go to the publisher and rectify the situation.

Once a copy of *A Boy's Will* had been retrieved, the two poets settled down in Pound's flat and the younger poet studied Frost's poems. "You don't mind our liking this, do you?" Pound asked. "Oh, no, go right ahead," Frost replied. [Parini, 128] Pound offered to review the book and kicked Frost out of his apartment so that he could begin work immediately. He also arranged for Frost to meet the Irish poet William Butler Yeats, whose work Frost had admired for decades.

When *A Boy's Will* was published in April of 1913, early reviews were mixed, contributing to a depression that settled on Frost for several weeks. By late May, his mood had lightened, and, returning from two weeks of family vacation in Scotland, found many positive reviews of *A Boy's Will* from both England and America.

Throughout that summer and into the fall, Robert Frost worked to complete *North of Boston*, his second volume of poetry. While some of his selections were created during his years on the New Hampshire farm, Frost wrote most of the poems in England, drawing on vivid memories of rural New England life. Much to Frost's frustration, Mrs. Nutt postponed the publication of *North of Boston* until the spring of 1914, but in the meantime, he met Edward Thomas, a man many consider to have been Frost's closest friend.

Thomas and Frost, of approximately the same age, both wrestled with depression, and public appreciation for their writing was slow in coming. When they met in October 1913, Thomas had established a reputation as a literary critic and nature writer, but Frost recognized the poetry in Thomas's prose and encouraged his friend to turn his efforts in that direction. Frost was frustrated with Ezra Pound's patronizing and arrogance, although he realized the good opinion of the established poet was essential to his success. In Thomas, Frost had discovered a man who approached him as an equal.

Frost and Thomas encouraged each other throughout the next year. The two writers shared an interest in rural speech and a belief that poetry should use common language and a natural voice. This position was a major departure from most poetry of their day, which featured elevated language. It sometimes forced words into awkward constructions so that a line would follow a particular pattern of rhyme or meter.

Frost feared that critics would dismiss his poetry as primitive because of its apparent simplicity, without recognizing the sophisticated treatment he was giving the language. In part to demonstrate that he knew what he was doing, he formulated a theory he called "the sound of sense." Sound was the spoken voice, giving life to the sense or meaning of the words. In a letter to an American friend, he expanded his theory:

> The best place to get the abstract sound of sense is from voices behind a door that cuts off the words . . . [Such] sounds are summoned by the audile imagination, and they must be positive, strong, and definitely and unmistakenly indicated by the context. . . . The sound of sense, then. You get that. It is the abstract vitality of our speech. It is pure sound, pure form. [Walsh, 120–121]

He further insisted that a poem that could not be listened to was doomed to oblivion:

> The living part of a poem is the intonation entangled somehow in the syntax, idiom, and meaning of a sentence. It is only there for those who have heard it previously in conversation. It is not for us in any Greek or Latin poem because our ears have not been filled with the tones of Greek and Roman talk. It is the most volatile and at the same time important part of poetry. It goes and the language becomes a dead language, the poetry dead poetry. . . . Words exist in the mouth, not in books. [Parini, 135]

In letters and conversations, Frost continued to develop this idea.

After a very simple Christmas celebration—money was in short supply and Frost hadn't received a shilling from the sales of *A Boy's Will*—the Frost family moved to Gloucestershire in western England. Living in a thatched cottage, they were able to enjoy the full charm of rural England with an affordable yearly rent of $50—about one-fifth of what they had been paying for the bungalow.

On May 15, 1914, *North of Boston* appeared on the literary scene. Many critics consider the volume to be Frost's finest collection, and it clearly established his poetic voice. Unlike his contemporaries—Pound, Yeats, T.S. Eliot, and Wallace Stevens—Frost showed no interest in urban life. He rarely wrote about historical events, friends, or the arts. Instead he focused almost exclusively on New England subsistence farming and, using images from this small, closed world, spoke universal truths in a new poetic language.

For two weeks, the book received no mention. Then a weak review appeared in the *Times Literary Supplement*. At last on June 13, the *Nation* printed a positive review. Citing "Mending Wall" and "Home Burial" the review tied Frost's originality to his ability to get "poetry back again into touch with the living vigours of speech . . . the rise and fall, the stressed pauses and little hurries, of spoken language." [Parini, 147] More positive reviews followed throughout the summer, encouraging Robert as he worked on poems for his third collection. However, he had mixed feelings about Ezra Pound's review, which appeared in a Chicago publication. While Pound praised Frost's work, he suggested that Frost was being published in England because American editors did not recognize his abilities. "I fear I am going to suffer a good deal at home by the support of Pound . . . ," Frost wrote to a friend. "Another such review as the one in *Poetry* and I shan't be admitted at Ellis Island. This is no joke." [Walsh, 207] Letters Frost received from American editors at the time reinforced his fears that Pound's review had offended them.

That summer, the Thomas family rented a farmhouse within sight of the Frosts' home, and the two writers often took walks together. No matter which path they chose, Thomas usually wished that they had taken the other. This quirk of his friend crystallized an idea Frost had been mulling over for months and led to his writing "The Road Not Taken," which opened his third volume of poetry, *Mountain Interval*.

In August, Britain declared war on Germany. At first Frost planned on sending his family back to the States, but perhaps lulled into security by the prevailing view that the war would be over by Christmas, he opted to keep his family where it was. His opinion began to change when he learned that

English publishers were cutting back on their poetry lists because of wartime supply shortages. Then in November, he received the news that Holt Publishing was releasing a trial run of *North of Boston* in America. "Now we can go home," Robert told Elinor. [Parini, 156]

He still held mixed feelings about leaving his friends in England, but on February 4, 1915 Germany announced that in two weeks the waters surrounding Great Britain would be a war zone and all ships in the area would be subject to submarine attack. At about the same time, a British merchant ship in the English Channel was torpedoed without warning. Short on money, Frost borrowed funds from friends to pay for his family's tickets on the American ship *St. Paul*, scheduled to leave Liverpool on February 13, 1915. Edward Thomas asked the Frosts to take his 15-year-old son, Mervyn, with them so that he could stay with relatives in New Hampshire, and the Frosts readily agreed.

As the date of their departure approached, Frost worried that he was leaving the only friends who had ever been truly supportive of his writing. He had no idea how his work would be received in America nor where and how his family would live, but because of the war, he felt he had to leave England. On the evening of February 13, the *St. Paul* left port. Passengers and crew alike feared German attack. The Frost family slept fully dressed, wearing their life jackets.

ESTABLISHING A REPUTATION

Once the *St. Paul* had broken free of European waters, the Frost family focused on the challenge of crossing the sea in rough winter weather. The constant pitching and rolling of the ship caused many passengers to be seasick, including the four Frost children. Nonetheless, Frost insisted that the family discuss where they would live once they returned to America. They quickly reached a consensus: they would stay as paying guests with friends in the Franconia region of New Hampshire while searching for a farm of their own.

The family landed in New York City on February 22, 1915. Mervyn Thomas was detained at Ellis Island because he was an immigrant, but the rest of the party settled in a hotel and went for a walk, enjoying the feel of solid land. When Frost stopped at a news stand and flipped through a copy of *The New Republic*, he was shocked to see a prominent review of *North of Boston*. The influential Amy Lowell described Frost's work as "the most American volume of poetry which has appeared for some time." [Parini, 160] An excited Frost quickly took advantage of the situation. Knowing that it would take a few days for Mervyn to settle immigration questions, Frost arranged for the rest of his family to take the train to New Hampshire while he visited the offices of Henry Holt Publishing. He learned from the head of the trade department that orders for *North of Boston* were pouring in. The man also gave the stunned poet a check for $40, payment from *The New Republic* for publishing "The Death of the Hired Man."

Eventually, Mervyn's immigration problems were settled, and Robert sent the young man by train to meet his New Hampshire relatives. Frost's own journey took a little longer. First he traveled to Pennsylvania to visit his sister, Jeanie. Finding her well, Frost headed north to Lawrence, Massachusetts, where he persuaded the family lawyer to give him an advance on his grandfather's annuity.

Stopping in Boston, Frost called on Ellery Sedgwick, editor of *The Atlantic Monthly*, who held enormous influence over the literary establishment. Editors had rejected Frost's earlier poetry submissions to *The Atlantic Monthly*, but now Sedgwick greeted the poet as a good friend. Sedgwick invited Frost to dinner and introduced the visitor to a number of Boston's well-known figures. Realizing that these connections might serve him well in the future, Frost extended his stay in Boston, leaving only after he had made a significant mark on the Boston literary society that held such power over the rest of the nation at that time.

After rejoining his family in New Hampshire, Frost began looking for a home and soon found the perfect farmhouse near Sugar Hill. The owner, however, had no interest in selling. Frost wouldn't take no for an answer, and the two men eventually agreed on a price of $1,000. Although it lacked indoor plumbing and electricity, the farm captured the imagination of the entire Frost family. They waited until June to move in, so that a carpenter could complete needed renovations.

In April, Frost ventured to Boston again for a poetry reading. During this visit, he met Louis Untermeyer, a young poet and critic, who became a close friend. He was happy to accept invitations from four private schools in the Boston area to give readings for $200 each—an honorarium equal to one-fifth of the sale price of his home. Although years had passed since he'd last taught, he enjoyed being in the classroom again. He used the opportunity to present his ideas about the importance of sound:

> When you listen to a speaker, you hear words, to be sure—but you also hear tones. The problem is to note them, to imagine them again, and to get them down in writing. But few of you probably ever thought of the possibility or of the necessity of doing this. You are generally told to distinguish simple, compound, and complex sentences—long and short—periodic

and loose—to vary sentence structure. . . .

. . . It is a fundamental fact that certain forms depend on the sound; e.g., note the various tones of irony, acquiescence, doubt, etc. in the farmer's "I guess so." And the great problem is, can you get those tones down on paper? How do you tell the tone? By the contact, by the animating spirit of the living voice. . . .

The vital thing, then, to consider in all composition, prose or verse, is the ACTION of the voice—sound-posturing, gesture. Get the stuff of life into the technique of your writing. That's the only escape from dry rhetoric. [Parini, 165–166]

That summer, Frost retreated to his home in New Hampshire and began writing for the first time in several months. The words came easily. Among the poems he produced are "Brown's Descent," "The Gum-Gatherer," "The Vanishing Red," and "'Out, Out—,'" which was based on the death of a friend's son. The boy died in 1901 after seriously injuring his hand in a sawing machine.

As Frost continued to produce poetry, his published poetry continued to find an enthusiastic audience. Ellery Sedgwick had decided to publish an essay about Frost in *The Atlantic Monthly*, as well as three poems: "Birches," "The Road Not Taken," and "The Sound of Trees". Holt notified the poet that a year and four printings after the trial release of *North of Boston*, the volume had sold 20,000 copies, an unheard of number for a book of poems. As Frost had feared, a small number of reviewers were offended that his poetry had first been published in England, but his American editor explained that Frost had "never offered a book to an American publisher" before he went abroad and "didn't cross the water seeking a British publisher." [Parini, 172]

Frost may have found it easier to ignore such reviews after William Dean Howells, a novelist and critic who had furthered the careers of Mark Twain and Henry James, praised Frost's work in *Harper's Monthly Magazine* in September of 1915. Howells was the most influential man of letters in the country and did not give endorsements lightly.

Everything seemed to be going well until that fall when Elinor, pregnant again, fell ill, and eventually miscarried. The children constantly fought colds, and Carol appeared to be developing tuberculosis or some other serious illness. Frost himself fought illness, brought on by fatigue from lecturing widely to generate income for his family. Throughout that winter and spring he spoke at private high schools, universities, and public gatherings, earning a reputation as entertaining and thought-provoking. In

June of 1916, the poet who loved irony was invited by Harvard to attend its commencement and read a poem. The Harvard dropout eagerly accepted.

That summer, Frost finished the arrangement of poems for *Mountain Interval*, which his American editor, Alfred Harcourt, asked about politely but insistently. Harcourt asked Holt's lawyers to review Frost's contract with David Nutt Publishing, which led to Frost's terminating that contract.

Two representatives of Amherst College in Amherst, Massachusetts visited Frost in the middle of the summer, inviting him to join the faculty in the spring semester of 1917. Frost wasn't sure anyone could teach writing, but he realized this move would provide a regular income and might improve the family's health by providing warmer living quarters for the winter. The New Hampshire farm could become a summer home.

In November of 1916, 42-year-old Frost saw his third collection of poems published with an initial printing of 4,000 copies—a very high number for a book of poetry at the time. While most critics agree that *North of Boston* is Frost's best book, *Mountain Interval* is known for four outstanding poems: "Birches," "The Road Not Taken," "Putting in the Seed," and "'Out, Out—'". Most reviewers praised Frost's writing, but the poet took personal umbrage at any comment he perceived as a slight, labeling unfavorable reviewers "enemies". He often viewed other contemporary poets as competitors and fell into the habit of making snide comments about them when their work was mentioned.

Frost suffered a genuinely devastating loss in the spring of 1917 with news of the death of his friend, Edward Thomas, who had joined the war in France. The English poet's wife wrote to Frost that his friend had been killed by a shell on the day after Easter. "Edward Thomas was the only brother I ever had," Frost confessed. "I fail to see how we can have been so much to each other, he an Englishman and I an American and our first meeting put off till we were both in middle life. I hadn't a plan for the future that didn't include him." [Parini, 179]

In spite of his grief, Frost continued teaching at Amherst, giving lectures, and socializing with editors, critics, and other poets. Because of his ambivalent feelings toward formal education, his classes were unlike any other college courses of the time. He never prepared lessons and frowned on assigning many projects or giving tests. He hated correcting papers, telling his students, "I'm not here to worry your writing into shape for you. Look to it yourself." [Meyers, 154] At the beginning of one class, he stated: "This is a class in seeing how long I can keep from reading what you write. Keep things till you have an accumulation and make a choice. . . . The first thing you show me this year is what you're going to get your mark on, so gird yourself and take your time. . . . I'm no perfunctory reader of perfunctory writing." [Meyers, 154]

Over the next couple years, life fell into a pattern. During the school year, Frost taught at Amherst. Summers were spent in New Hampshire. But increasingly, he wondered about the appropriateness of spending his energies teaching when he could be writing. These feelings became more acute after the fall of 1918 when he became seriously ill for 10 weeks, one of the thousands of victims of the infamous flu epidemic. He also disagreed with the political positions of the president of Amherst. Frost supported the United States entering the Great War in 1917 and objected to the president's socialist views which conflicted with Frost's own rugged individualism. The war ended in November 1918, but the differences between the two men became more noticeable, and in June of 1920 Frost left Amherst with no intention of returning.

That summer, Frost sold his farm in New Hampshire and settled his family on an old farm in southern Vermont, which the Frosts came to call Stone Cottage. Returning to country living immediately increased his writing output. Between 1917 and the first half of 1920, he wrote fewer than six poems; in the summer and fall of 1920, he wrote half a dozen important poems, including "The Star-Splitter" and "Fire and Ice," and also completed many previously unfinished works.

Life was not trouble free, however. In 1920, police in Portland, Maine, detained Jeanie for disturbing the peace, apparently dementedly; Frost committed his sister to a state-run mental hospital in Augusta, Maine, where she would live out her life. Frost seldom visited her because he found the encounters too painful. Without the regular paycheck from Amherst the family finances again became a challenge. Frost arranged to teach summer courses at Bread Loaf Mountain, where Middlebury College had just started a School of English. He was also invited by the University of Michigan to spend the 1921–1922 school year as a visiting fellow with an annual salary of $5000, an increase of 25 percent over that of his last year at Amherst.

Frost accepted the position, and for the first time, his family became scattered. The parents traveled to Ann Arbor, Michigan, with their older daughters, Lesley and Irma, who planned to audit courses at the university. Carol stayed at Stone Cottage to take care of the farm, and Marjorie lived with a friend in Vermont so that she could continue her high school education among students she knew. Frost's new position was largely created by him and involved little teaching. Instead he brought a series of writers to the school to lecture, gave public readings for the people of Ann Arbor, and worked with undergraduate writers. He managed to write a few poems—an improvement over the situation at Amherst—and began planning a fourth collection. At the end of the academic year, the president invited him to return, and Frost agreed.

That summer, he taught at Bread Loaf and worked on his collection *New Hampshire* with Lincoln MacVeagh, his new editor at Holt. Scheduled for release in the spring of 1923, the new book would be introduced along with an anthology of the best poems from Frost's first three books. MacVeagh thought this strategy would help establish the poet as a major contemporary figure. Unfortunately, a string of illnesses delayed the completion of the new volume.

Frost completed his second year at Michigan and accepted an offer to return to Amherst, where the president had recently been dismissed and several of the faculty had left in protest. He stipulated that he would teach only two classes a semester and be free to write the remainder of the time.

In the summer of 1923, Carol married his sister Marjorie's best friend, Lillian LaBatt. The older Frosts left the new couple on the Vermont farm while they moved to Amherst and prepared for the fall semester and a series of speaking engagements.

When *New Hampshire* was published on November 15, 1923, it quickly earned good reviews. Among the most admired poems in the collection are "Fire and Ice," "Stopping by Woods on a Snowy Evening," "The Aim Was Song," and "To Earthward." The collection earned Robert Frost the Pulitzer Prize for Poetry in 1924, further enhancing his public reputation. As he prepared to return to Amherst that fall, though, he already was planning to leave.

CHANGING TIMES

In November 1924, the *Boston Evening Transcript* made public Frost's secret that he'd accepted a lifelong fellowship at the University of Michigan and would be leaving Amherst at the end of the school year. No one could question why the poet accepted this position. The school would provide all his living expenses and require no teaching. Frost was asked simply to write.

When he left for Michigan in the fall of 1925, he looked forward to weeks of writing. But the fellowship at Michigan evolved into something quite different. Frost soon became the center of a social whirl of dinners and speaking engagements that kept him too busy for writing. "When I sit down to write I must see before me a few days of undisturbed concentration," he told a local reporter. [Meyers, 172] Those "few days" constantly eluded him. Both Frosts hated being so far from their adult children. In a letter to his friend John Bartlett, Frost wrote:

> I am not sure of hanging on long at Ann Arbor though the
> position is supposed to be for life. It's too far from the children
> for the stretch of our heart strings. . . . We've just come on to be
> with Marj for an operation for appendicitis. . . . What I want is a
> farm in New England once more. [Meyers, 172]

After Marjorie's surgery, Elinor stayed in Massachusetts while Frost returned
to Ann Arbor. Alone, he worried that he was not producing much poetry,
realizing that when poets stopped writing, they were often dismissed as "has-
beens". When the president of Amherst offered $5,000 a year for just ten
weeks of teaching, Frost quickly accepted. His lifetime fellowship at the
University of Michigan had lasted all of one academic year.

When school ended that spring, Frost rejoined Elinor at their Vermont
farm, which now boasted an additional 100 apple trees as a result of son
Carol's labors. Marjorie continued to recover from her surgery, and Lillian,
Carol's wife, was extremely ill, requiring surgery in July. The summer
became more complicated when Irma announced she was marrying a Kansas
farmer and would join him on his family farm. Exhausted from performing
work that normally would have been done by Marjorie and Lillian, Elinor
decided she and her husband needed a break. They vacationed in New
Hampshire until the end of October.

The rest did wonders for Frost's writing. He totally reworked "West-
Running Brook," begun six years earlier, which combines the two poetic
forms Frost used most: dramatic (telling a story) and lyric (using something
in nature as a metaphor for the poet's emotions or ideas about life).

Following Irma's November wedding, Frost began another lecture tour.
His public appearances had become a mainstay of his life. They produced a
sizeable income and kept him in the public eye, two things very important to
a man who hadn't achieved critical acclaim until age 40. "It is a miserable
business being a poet among professors and business men," he told his friend
John Bartlett. "The only way to make them respect you is to make them pay."
[Meyers, 182]

Lucrative as these tours were, they exacted a great amount of energy. A
man who enjoyed solitude, Frost found it taxing to interact with crowds of
people he didn't know. Traveling hundreds of miles by train, sleeping in
strange beds in cheap motels, and eating institutional food at odd hours
fatigued him. He also had to face the terror of public speaking. Although
experience had taught him to mask his discomfort, he never lost the fear he
first exhibited while speaking at his high school graduation. And he never
stopped expressing his agitation by complaining to his hosts. If a large
audience arrived, Frost fretted that the auditorium was too small. If a smaller

group gathered, he worried that his fame had ended and that he would never be invited to speak again. Success did not bring greater confidence. Frost believed each accomplishment simply raised people's expectations and delayed inevitable failure.

In spite of his self-doubt, Frost excelled as a public speaker. He had a good sense of humor, spoke with an unerring sense of drama, and showed excellent timing. These skills captivated audiences even in informal settings. One student described a philosophy class Frost was invited to attend:

> Frost began to discuss metaphors in an easy way, asking occasional questions to bring out ideas. Gradually the evening shadows lengthened and after a while Frost alone was talking. The room grew darker and darker until we could not see each others' faces. But no one even thought of turning on the light. The dinner hour came and went, and still no one of that half score of hungry boys dreamed of leaving. We dared not even stir for fear of interrupting. Finally, long after seven, Frost stopped and said, "Well, I guess that's enough." We thanked him and left as if under a spell. [Parini, 243]

During such lectures, Frost became known for voicing unexpected opinions. One time he learned that the poet W.D. Snodgrass had told students at Wayne State University that Frost's poem "Stopping by Woods on a Snowy Evening" alluded to suicide. When Frost later addressed the Wayne State students, Snodgrass recalled, "He talked about how scandalous it was that certain academics would say such things about him and his work." [Meyers, 184] The next day, Frost spoke in Ann Arbor, Michigan, and reportedly said of the poem, "Well, now, that does have a good deal of the ultimate about it, doesn't it?" [Meyers, 184] If that account is accurate, it is a marked departure from Frost's usual pronouncements about "Stopping by Woods". He repeatedly proclaimed that the poem had nothing to do with death.

Frost came home from his 1927 lecture tour physically and emotionally exhausted, unable to write for weeks. Elinor wished he would stop speaking altogether, and this subject became a constant source of conflict. She once told their daughter Lesley: "Your father *must* give this up. His health is failing. His life is being ruined. His poetry is suffering. It *can't* go on." [Meyers, 187] But go on it did, although Frost confessed in a letter, "I should have got off the train somewhere coming east and taken a month and ten days in some likely desert all by myself for a rest from smiling at my fellow man." [Meyers, 187]

Worries at home also weighed on the poet. Marjorie's health continued to fail, and Carol and Lillian constantly struggled with financial and health problems. Conflict in Irma's marriage caused her to leave her husband in Kansas and take their infant son to the Vermont farm. These problems periodically brought on weeks and months of depression. "One could easily imagine him subsiding, never leaving his bedroom," Frost's friend Victor Reichert observed years later. "But teaching, and the public readings—these demands were crucial. They kept him from withdrawing. He knew that, of course. He was self-protective in this way. He used the demands of his public career to keep himself afloat." [Parini, 244]

In the summer of 1928, the Frosts decided a change in climate might improve Marjorie's health. Their friend Dorothy Canfield Fisher, a novelist, knew a family in Sèvres, a small town outside Paris, and arranged for Marjorie to visit. On August 4, 1928, they set sail for France, arriving a week later. Frost tolerated a few days of sightseeing in Paris before he and Elinor accompanied Marjorie to Sèvres, but he remained worried and confided in a letter to his English friend John Haines that they saw no improvement in Marjorie and the disappointment "has been almost too much for Elinor on top of everything else she has had to bear for the last two years". [Parini, 252]

As soon as they had left Marjorie in Sèvres, the Frosts traveled to England to reunite with some of their old friends as well as to fulfill a longstanding wish to visit Ireland. A highlight of Frost's travels in Ireland was meeting with the poet William Butler Yeats. Back in England, they visited many literary acquaintances and were the overnight guests of the poet Walter de la Mare and his wife. "De la Mare is the best of the best," Frost reported in a letter to an American friend. [Parini, 254–255] They also visited Helen Thomas, the widow of Frost's close friend Edward.

Frost made note of everything with his usual dry sense of humor. In one letter, the 54-year-old poet described his reaction to a friend's poem: "He has since sent me a poem in which he stoutly excuses us all for looking so horribly old after such a terrible war. . . . I don't want to be excused for looking horribly old. I want it denied I look horribly old." [Parini, 255]

On October 19, Frost attended a dinner party with T.S. Eliot, an American poet who had become a naturalized British citizen the previous year. While the poets maintained polite conversation throughout the meal, Frost was unimpressed with Eliot's acquired English accent, and "considered him a snob, and a fake," said Richard Eberhart. "Those were the worst things you could be in Frost's way of thinking." [Parini, 256]

Frost, Elinor, and Marjorie set sail for America on November 15. While Frost was at sea, Holt published his fifth volume of poetry, *West-Running Brook*. It received mixed reviews because its overall quality was not quite as high as *New Hampshire* and because Frost's pastoral poetry was so different from the poetry of contemporaries such as Carl Sandburg and T.S. Eliot. Still, Frost had included some important works in this newest collection, including the title poem, "Spring Pools," "Acquainted with the Night," and "Once by the Pacific," one of his few poems that drew on childhood experiences in California.

Back in America, new challenges arose. Marjorie wanted to study nursing, but her parents worried that her health would not hold up under the heavy course load. Irma's marriage continued to have problems, and the Frosts discovered that Lesley had married while they were in Europe and almost immediately encountered serious disagreements with her husband on a number of issues. Then in 1929, Jeanie died in the mental hospital in which she had lived for nine years.

These personal problems contributed to Frost's inability to produce much poetry. They also increased his anxiety over how *Collected Poems*, a compilation of his previous five books, would be received when it was published in 1930. The book would embody most of his life's work, and he viewed its reviews as judgments of his overall writing skill. Many of the first reviews were quite negative. Granville Hicks, an important critic, wrote in *The New Republic* that the poems contained "nothing of industrialism." Hicks also noted that Frost could not "give us the sense of belonging in the industrial, scientific, Freudian world in which we find ourselves." [Parini, 267]

Incensed at being thought out of step with his times, Frost was only slightly mollified by the stream of positive reviews that followed. Later in that year, the news that he had been earned his second Pulitzer Prize for Poetry stunned him. On November 13, he was elected to the prestigious American Academy of Arts and Letters. *Collected Poems* secured Robert Frost's reputation as an important American poet.

Family troubles quickly overshadowed the joy of these achievements. Marjorie contracted tuberculosis and entered a sanitarium in Boulder, Colorado. The following spring, Carol's wife, Lillian, also contracted tuberculosis. Both women recovered, but only after years of treatment.

In Boulder, Marjorie met Willard Fraser, an archeologist. Frost met the man in 1932 and liked him immensely, calling him "as good as his letters." [Parini, 283] The couple planned to marry in 1933. For the moment, Frost felt encouraged. Lillian and Marjorie were regaining their health. His income from teaching, lectures, and royalties protected him from the hard times so many Americans were experiencing during the Great Depression and allowed him to buy a large home in Amherst, where he continued to teach 10 weeks each year. His favorite daughter planned to marry a man of whom he thoroughly approved. The happiness would not last.

THE CRUCIBLE

In the months leading up to Marjorie's wedding, Frost suffered a bad case of the flu. After briefly recovering, he immersed himself in teaching and resumed his usual round of speaking engagements, but he again fell ill, this time seriously. By the end of May he was bedridden, and the doctor feared tuberculosis. Tuberculosis was ruled out, but a series of respiratory ailments and fevers plagued Frost throughout the summer and seasonal allergies added further complications. In June, he barely made it to Montana for Marjorie's wedding and his condition forced cancellations of scheduled appearances in the late summer and fall of 1933.

As 1934 began, Frost had regained his health and was teaching. Elinor traveled to Billings, Montana, to be with Marjorie, who was expecting a baby in March. The baby, Marjorie Robin Fraser, was born on March 16. Two weeks later, Elinor rushed back to Massachusetts because Frost had suffered a relapse. Almost immediately after her arrival, the Frosts received news that Marjorie had become infected with puerperal fever and was delirious. The worried parents left for Billings and arranged for Marjorie to be transported to the Mayo Clinic in Rochester, Minnesota. Doctors there offered a new treatment for the usually fatal infection, but Marjorie did not respond. Her fever reached 110 degrees. On May 2, 1934, she died.

Devastated, the 60-year-old Frost wrote to his friend Louis Untermeyer: "The blow has fallen. The noblest of us all is dead and has taken our hearts out of the world with her. It was a terrible seven weeks' fight—too indelibly terrible on the imagination. . . .We were torn afresh every day between the temptation to let her go untortured or cruelly trying to save her." [Meyers, 204]

Elinor felt Marjorie's death more keenly than she had that of her son Elliot 34 years earlier. "With Robert I have to keep cheerful, because I mustn't drag him down," she wrote to a close friend, "but sometimes it seems to me that I *cannot* go on any longer. . . . I long to die myself and be relieved of the pain that I feel for her sake." [Meyers, 204]

Carol Frost and his family—his wife, Lillian, and their son, Prescott—arrived from California. Marjorie's now widowed husband, Willard, was so overwhelmed with grief that he could not care for his newborn daughter. Elinor and Lillian took over. The work was too much for Elinor, and in November she suffered a serious heart attack. Following the doctor's advice, the extended family moved to Key West, Florida, for the winter. With no improvement in Elinor's condition, Frost wrote to Amherst and explained that he would be unable to teach. When the couple returned to Amherst in April of 1935, he tried to make up for his earlier absence by plunging into a series of well-attended lectures and readings in the community. That summer, the Frosts made a painful trip to Montana to visit Willard and their grandchild.

Back in Vermont in the fall, Frost began thinking about a new book of poems. As he had with all his previous books, he dedicated the volume to Elinor. First he submitted several poems to major periodicals. As a result, about half the poems that would later be published in *A Further Range* first appeared in magazines in 1936. "You see, I have to keep reminding them I'm here," Frost told Untermeyer. [Parini, 300]

In October of 1935, Elinor's chest pains became more severe, and the doctor recommended moving to a warmer climate that would place less strain on her heart. The president of Amherst again excused Frost from teaching. When Frost himself became ill that winter, Elinor took care of him although she was in worse health than he.

In the spring of 1936, Frost gave several interviews in which he expressed his conservative political views. He disagreed with President Franklin D. Roosevelt's policies and opposed the talk of communism, industrial conflict, and social welfare that was so popular among many American writers of the time. He also aired these views while at Harvard in March to give the Charles Eliot Norton lectures. Frost's political pronouncements were not appreciated by Harvard's president, but they received a much more sympathetic hearing from an old acquaintance, professor Ted Morrison, and his wife, Kay. The couple hosted formal receptions for Frost that official Harvard failed to provide.

When *A Further Range*, Frost's sixth book, was published on May 29, his well-known political opinions influenced many critics, who gave the book negative reviews. While the book had more mediocre poems than his earlier efforts, it also contained fine examples of poetry, including the sonnet "Design," which many authorities consider to be Frost's greatest poem. Critics, however, chose to focus on the weaker politically pointed poems, such as "Build Soil". University of Chicago Professor Morton Zabel wrote in the *Southern Review* that "uncritical indulgence [had] owed pieces of dull writing and petulant wisdom to enter this volume." [Meyers, 219] Another reviewer concluded that "the diction [was] faded, the expression imprecise, and the tone extraordinarily tired and uneasy." [Meyers, 219]

As the negative reviews piled up, Robert spiraled into depression. He canceled almost all his speaking engagements for late summer and early fall and failed to teach classes at Amherst. A painful attack of shingles exacerbated his depression, and by late November he wrote to a friend, "Too much has happened to me this year. I am stopped in my tracks as if everybody in the opposing eleven had concentrated on me." [Parini, 307]

Late in that year, Frost decided he needed to re-engage the outside world. He began by attending a Christmas family reunion in San Antonio, Texas. Positive reviews, partly in reaction to the harsh critiques of the summer, began to appear in important publications, and in May of 1937 Frost was awarded his third Pulitzer Prize for Poetry, an unprecedented achievement. The book sold well, making him the best-selling American poet since Henry Wadsworth Longfellow.

Elinor used these events to strengthen her argument that Frost should return to speaking and teaching. In that fall, he began to lecture, but he avoided teaching because of Elinor's continued health problems. In spite of that worry, the family enjoyed a large Christmas dinner in Gainesville Florida. The Frosts provided apartments for Carol and Lesley and their families so that everyone could be together, and Lesley handled the cooking and cleaning that Elinor was far too weak to attempt. At the beginning of 1938, Frost was encouraged by favorable reviews and by March he was ready to write again.

In mid-March, Frost took Elinor to visit a house in Gainesville that they were interested in buying. On the way home, they discussed making an offer. Once they returned to their apartment building, Elinor headed up the stairs toward their second-floor entrance. Halfway there, she dropped to her knees, suffering a major heart attack. Over the next two days, she experienced seven more heart attacks. Because Frost was so upset, the doctor did not allow him to see Elinor, fearing his presence would further exhaust the critically ill woman. On March 20, 1938, Elinor died. The only woman Frost had ever loved, his wife for 43 years, was gone.

Lesley accused her father of failing as a father and husband and of speeding Elinor's death by allowing her to take the upstairs apartment. His daughter's charges combined with his overwhelming grief and feelings of guilt about the hardships Elinor had endured during their marriage pushed Frost into a deep depression. A serious respiratory illness compounded his misery. Anything associated with Elinor caused him great pain, so he sold his home in Amherst. The loss also strengthened his resolve to resign from the college. Amherst's president accepted the decision with regret but failed to offer to retain him as professor emeritus, an omission that deepened Frost's sense of being cut off from the world.

Frost retreated to Vermont, but his home there was "too full of Elinor to withstand," so he temporarily moved in with Carol and his family. [Parini, 313] Concerned by Frost's isolation, Ted Morrison invited him to lecture at the Bread Loaf Writers' Conference in Vermont that August. Frost agreed and lectured to an enthusiastic audience, but his grief caused him to behave erratically and drink heavily—something he rarely did because of his father's problems with alcohol.

That summer, Frost began a romantic relationship with Ted Morrison's wife, Kay. She refused to marry him, but she did agree to act as his personal secretary and manager. She became the inspiration behind his writing. People differ over the exact nature of this relationship. Some believe Kay was Frost's mistress for the rest of his life; others hold that the romantic element was short-lived. Whatever is true, Ted tolerated the relationship, and most people agree that it saved Frost's sanity. Frost himself wrote to the couple shortly after the conference: "You two rescued me from a very dangerous self when you had the idea of keeping me for the whole session at Bread Loaf. I am still infinitely restless, but I came away from you as good as saved." [Parini, 316]

Frost felt better, but he was clearly not back to normal. Friends noticed his odd behavior, and he lacked his usual spark during public appearances. In September, he moved to Boston, where Kay quickly imposed order on the chaos of his correspondence. But throughout that fall and winter, he suffered from respiratory illnesses, one of which necessitated hospitalization. A visit with his son, Carol, left Frost profoundly disturbed. Carol felt like a failure and was embarrassed by his constant need for financial help from his father.

The new year was not without hope, however. In January, Holt published Frost's *Collected Poems*, and he received the Gold Medal for Poetry from the National Institute of Arts and Letters. Throughout the spring of 1939, Frost traveled to various speaking engagements. Those who worked with him noted that he seemed exhausted and unusually irritable. When he returned to Boston in May, he received an invitation from Harvard to become a Ralph Waldo Emerson Fellow—a two-year appointment with no formal duties. Frost accepted the position, although he had reservations about becoming tied to a university once more.

Frost spent the summer in Vermont and purchased a farm near Bread Loaf so that he could easily remain involved in the writers' conference. He lived in a cabin on the farm while Ted and Kay Morrison stayed in the main house.

Life seemed to be returning to normal for Frost that fall as he dove into activities at Harvard, but illness and depression continued to plague him. He was also worried about Carol, and bought some property in Florida in hopes that his son would be able to oversee its development. Unfortunately Carol's problems were much more severe than his father guessed. In early October of 1940, Carol's wife, Lillian, asked Frost to join them at the Vermont farm. She was scheduled for surgery and feared leaving her extremely depressed husband alone with 16-year-old Prescott.

Frost was alarmed by Carol's condition and, fearing his son was suicidal, stayed with him for days until he was convinced the crisis had passed. He left for his home in Cambridge on October 8, but at 7:00 A.M. the next day he received a call from Prescott, who had been awakened by the sound of a gunshot to find his father lying in a pool of blood on the kitchen floor, dead.

"I took the wrong way with [Carol]," Frost wrote to Louis Untermeyer. "I tried many ways and every single one of them was wrong. Some thing in me is still asking for the chance to try one more. There's where the greatest pain is located. I am cut off too abruptly in my plans and efforts for his peace of mind." [Parini, 332] Within six years, Frost had lost his favorite daughter, his wife, and his son. The pain of these losses would contribute to some of his best poetry in years.

A New Beginning

Over the next few years, Frost taught at Harvard and spoke throughout the country. He bought a home in Cambridge, Massachusetts and became a familiar figure in the university town, walking with his black-and-white Border Collie, Gillie.

He was also quietly gathering poems for another book. Some of the poems were revisions of works from decades earlier, such as "A Subverted Flower," which he had refrained from publishing before because its explicitly represented sexuality clearly referred to Elinor. Others were more recent, such as "The Gift Outright," which, while technically accomplished, has lost some of its popularity in recent years because it ignores the fact that North America was inhabited by Native Americans long before Europeans arrived. Frost also chose poems that reflected his love and respect for Kay Morrison, such as "The Silken Tent," a one-sentence sonnet strongly influenced by Shakespeare. Some poems exuded joy; others hinted at struggles the poet had faced. Titled *A Witness Tree*, this collection of 42 poems, first appeared on April 23, 1942, and was dedicated "To K.M. for her part in it."

The book generally received praise from critics, although they noted that many of the poems were not up to the standard of the best works within its pages. Two months after the book's release, Holt had sold more than 10,000 copies. The nation had entered World War II a few months before, and many readers appreciated the tone of "The Gift Outright." Frost himself was ambivalent about the war. Before the United States became directly involved, he objected to the idea that Americans should protect the British, but after the Japanese attack on Pearl Harbor he became more sympathetic toward the war effort. His son-in-law Willard Fraser and his grandson

Prescott enlisted. Unlike many artists of his day, however, Frost refused to produce propaganda materials.

The poet also worried about finances. A renegotiated contract with his publisher Holt and an agreement to sell original manuscripts to a collector guaranteed Frost a comfortable living, but he never felt entirely secure. To add to his concerns, Harvard had an all-male student body, and most young men were enlisting. This cut the number of students and reduced the financial resources of the university. Frost became an honorary faculty member but no longer received a salary. He also continued to disagree with the university's president over many political and philosophical ideas; and in 1943 he accepted a position at Dartmouth in Hanover, New Hampshire. In spite of his unpleasant student days, his memory of the school was warm. Conveniently, his daughter Irma and her family also lived in Hanover.

Before Frost ventured to Dartmouth, he received news that he had been awarded the Pulitzer Prize for Poetry for *A Witness Tree*, in spite of the feelings of some members of the prize committee that no one should receive the award four times.

Rather than live in Hanover, Frost remained based in Cambridge, where Kay Morrison continued to organize his life and handle many of his business arrangements. He took the train from Boston to Dartmouth each Friday and taught on Friday, Saturday, and Sunday, returning to Boston at the beginning of the week. He also continued his pattern of spending the winter in Florida and the summer in Vermont.

While at Dartmouth, Robert began working on two verse plays: *A Masque of Reason* and *A Masque of Mercy*. While neither play is considered an important part of his writing, both works reflect his attempts to work through his personal losses. *A Masque of Reason* presents itself as an additional chapter to the Old Testament Book of Job, which deals with the question of why God allows suffering. *A Masque of Mercy* is more allegorical and deals with the question of divine justice.

A Masque of Reason was published in March of 1945, as the war in Europe appeared to be resolving in an Allied victory. Most reviews were quite critical, and even Frost's supporters were hard pressed to be enthusiastic. The majority of critics sided with poet Louise Bogan, who wrote in *The New Yorker*, "Frost, bringing us up against the problem of Pain and Evil, adds nothing to our insight on the subject." [Meyers, 280] People paid particular attention to Frost's handling of pain and evil because the past six years had been filled with horrific images from the war and the worst atrocities of the German concentration camps.

Such reviews could not damage Frost's popularity, however. Across the nation, people of all ages thronged to his readings and lectures. As soldiers returned from the war and enrolled in colleges, Dartmouth found its enrollment growing, and students competed to get into his classes. The poet also stole time to continue refining *A Masque of Mercy* and to prepare some of his most recent poems for publication in the book *Steeple Bush.*

In 1946, Irma's husband divorced her. Emotionally unstable for years, she had become so paranoid that doctors believed she would not be able to live on her own for much longer. With memories of Carol's suicide still fresh, Frost feared his daughter was headed toward the same end and also worried that she was much too dependent on her six-year-old son, Harold. Nevertheless, he and Kay complied with Irma's request that they find a home for her near her father. They settled the troubled woman and her son in Acton, Massachusetts—near enough to Cambridge to make contact easy, but far enough away so that Irma would not constantly visit her father.

In early May of 1947, just after his return to Cambridge from his annual winter stay in Florida, Frost was surprised one day to find T.S. Eliot at his doorstep. "I was in town and I couldn't leave without coming to pay my respects," Eliot announced. [Meyers, 306] He chose to ignore the unflattering things Frost had said about him on the lecture circuit, and instead the two poets discussed their days in England and their works-in-progress.

They also discussed the problems faced by Ezra Pound, the American poet both had known while living in England before World War I. A fanatical follower of Italian dictator Benito Mussolini, Pound had been arrested for making treasonous broadcasts on Italian radio during World War II. In 1945, a panel of psychiatrists, attempting to protect Pound from punishment, judged him unfit to stand trial, and the poet was confined at St. Elizabeth's Hospital for the Criminally Insane in Washington, D.C.

As the visit between Frost and Eliot drew to a close, Frost found himself feeling better toward the other poet than he had in decades. Years later, Frost told an acquaintance, "Eliot is my friend. . . . Our friends always try to make us enemies, to no avail." [Meyers, 307]

Later that month, Holt published *Steeple Bush*, which was dedicated to Frost's six grandchildren, and the poet spent the summer in Vermont, dreading the inevitable reviews. "They always get it wrong," he once told an interviewer while discussing critics. [Parini, 369] In general reviewers treated *Steeple Bush* kindly, although they recognized that it fell short of the overall quality of his earlier collections. Most recognized "Directive" as the strongest work in the book. Later that year, poet and critic Randall Jarrell published his essay "The Other Frost" in which he identified the dark side of Frost's poetry. Most reviewers, however, oversimplified the poet's work.

Liberals pointed to his political ideas when criticizing his work, while conservatives attacked him for lacking any moral point of view.

As the summer of 1947 drew to a close, Irma's deteriorating mental condition reached a crisis. One day in August, she left her home in Acton and aimlessly wandered the streets of Cambridge, eventually landing on her father's doorstep. Frost was in Vermont, but Carol's widow, Lillian, was at the Cambridge house. Recognizing Irma's extreme anxiety levels, Lillian persuaded her sister-in-law to come in. Then she alerted Frost about the situation and, that evening, Kay drove the poet back to Cambridge. Fearful that Irma might endanger his seven-year-old grandson, Frost followed the advice of friend and psychiatrist Merrill Moore and committed Irma to the state mental hospital in Concord, New Hampshire.

The decision created more turmoil in his family. Still angry at her father about her mother's death and other issues, Lesley blamed her father for placing her sister in an asylum even though she herself would not take care of Irma. "Cast your eye back over my family luck," Frost later said to his friend Untermeyer, "and perhaps you will wonder if I haven't had pretty near enough." [Meyers, 288]

Professional disappointment soon compounded Frost's personal sorrows. In October, *A Masque of Mercy* appeared, and most reviews were scathing. Writing in *Partisan Review*, Leslie Fiedler called the play "[a] bad book, shallow, corny, and unmercifully cute." [Meyers, 281] But late in that fall, Amherst President Charles Cole offered Frost the position of Simpson Lecturer in Literature, to take effect in 1949. It required only that he give one lecture and one reading a year. Frost agreed to a five-year contract paying $3,500 per year, more than the average U.S. family made. When the contract expired, he would receive an annual retirement allowance of $2,500. Robert Frost would end his college teaching career where it had begun.

In 1949, as Frost approached his 75th birthday, Holt prepared to publish *Complete Poems of Robert Frost 1949*. This volume included the original text of each of Frost's previously published manuscripts—from *A Boy's Will* (1913) to *Steeple Bush* (1947). It also contained three recent poems as well as his two masques. The publication of *Complete Poems* launched a decade filled with honors and unique challenges for the man who was arguably America's best-loved poet.

A Season of Honors

The release of *Complete Poems* opened a floodgate of public recognition. The U.S. Senate passed a resolution on March 26, 1950, offering him the "felicitations of the Nation which he has served so well." [Meyers, 293] *Time* joined other publications in praising *Complete Poems* and then followed up with an October 9, 1950 cover story on Frost. "Of living U.S. poets," *Time*'s article stated, "none has lodged poems more surely where they will be hard to get rid of." [Parini, 381] According to the article, Frost's work had sold more than 375,000 copies, an figure never before heard of in poetry.

Although Frost had never earned an undergraduate degree, he held dozens of honorary degrees, gaining on average one a year from 1918 to 1962. With his honorary doctorates he received brightly colored hoods to wear with the requisite graduation gown, symbolizing the degree he had been awarded. By 1955, he had such a stash of hoods that he decided to find a practical use for them and had them cut up and sewn into a patchwork quilt.

Although showered with adulation, in 1950 Frost wrote in a notebook, "There is a shadow on success." He continued to suffer from depression, which he termed "a daily gloominess," and even attending small dinners cost the old poet great amounts of energy. "You could sense the strain, even with the brilliance," one friend observed. [Parini, 382]

With Kay Morrison's help, Frost continued to carve out times of solitude when he would sit writing in his old Morris chair with a book board stretched across its arms. While he produced far less poetry than he had in earlier years, he did create new works. In his notebooks from that period, he wrote, "We'll have to have a new book pretty soon again only to show our development hasn't been arrested by prosperity. Kay says so." [Parini, 384] While a book wasn't immediately forthcoming, in the summer of 1953, Frost wrote "Kitty Hawk," which he considered to be the most important poem of his last decade.

Frost did not see old age as an acceptable excuse for withdrawing from life. He felt a responsibility to younger poets, especially the men, whom he had always found easier to relate to than women. The notable exception was Adrienne Rich, with whom he got along extremely well. He particularly prized his relationship with the young poet Robert Lowell, a cousin of Amy Lowell who had helped establish Frost's career in America. Robert Lowell suffered from mental illness, a fact that disturbed many of his friends, but Frost, with so much experience with mental illness in his own family, took Lowell's breakdowns in stride, encouraging visits from the younger man and visiting him when he was hospitalized.

Frost's strong opinions did not diminish with age, however, and he detested the work of some younger poets, particularly Dylan Thomas and Allen Ginsberg. Of Ginsberg, he told friends that he had "read only Ginsberg's *Howl.* . . . It's not very good—just a pouring out. Anyone can do it. . . . *Howl* is not real: one can't howl on for so many pages." [Meyers, 297]

Robert Frost also continued to meet with his peers. He often had dinner or afternoon tea with Harvard professor I. A. Richards, a powerful literary critic and theorist. The meal would be followed by hours of conversation. "[Frost] had an unusually theoretical mind," Richards later recalled, "and like[d] to talk about language and meaning. . . . 'Poets were the historians of language', he said. He knew vast stretches of English and American poetry by heart, and reached easily for examples in his conversation. I was always startled by his verbatim recall of poets from Shakespeare through Tennyson." [Parini, 384]

On March 25, 1954, Frost's longtime publisher Holt hosted a lavish dinner in honor of the poet's 80th birthday. It was preceded by a three-hour news conference at the Waldorf-Astoria Hotel in New York City. Two dozen reporters peppered Frost with questions while he sat under hot lights before a dozen television cameras. The dinner that evening was also held at the hotel, and the guest list included poets, critics, senators, and jurists.

On the next day—his actual birthday—Frost traveled to Amherst, where the college sponsored a black-tie dinner in his honor. After the meal, Frost received the watercolor *Winter Sunlight* by the New England artist Andrew Wyeth, with whom he had become friends. After a host of friends, including Archibald MacLeish and Louis Untermeyer, praised the poet's accomplishments and artistry, Frost himself stood to speak. In response to the compliments that had been showered upon him all evening, he observed, "People say you're this and you're that and you wonder if you're anything. All I've wanted to do is to write a few little poems it'd be hard to get rid of. That's all I ask." [Parini, 391]

That summer, Frost's daughter Lesley persuaded him to attend the World Congress of Writers in São Paulo, Brazil, but only after a considerable effort to overcome her father's marked lack of interest in traveling to non–English-speaking nations. The 80-year-old man agreed because it pleased him to have Lesley interested in doing something with him and because the Eisenhower administration presented the idea to him as a patriotic duty that might help improve U.S. relations with Brazil. Lesley, who had made several trips to South America, would be her father's interpreter. Organizers had invited the United States government to send one poet and one novelist. William Faulkner was selected as the American novelist.

Father and daughter left for Brazil on August 4. The journey took 24 hours, and they were exhausted when they arrived. Frost did not look forward to meeting Faulkner, whose writing he detested. The two American writers barely saw each other because Faulkner was usually drunk in his hotel room. "It was as I feared with Faulkner," he wrote to Kay. "He has stolen the show by doing nothing for it but to lie up dead drunk like a genius. The consul . . . has been caring for Faulkner day and night, bathing him in the tub and feeding him in bed. . . . He looked very sick and ashamed to me." [Meyers, 295]

But the enthusiastic crowds greeting Frost wherever he went energized him. American poet Elizabeth Bishop lived in Brazil at the time and had concluded from gossip that Frost must be a "malicious old bore". After she attended a reading, however, she praised him in a letter to friends: "Frost did marvelously, of course—the Brazilians got his every joke. . . . He gave a reading at the Embassy. . . . He is amazing for a man eighty years old, and the audience—mostly Brazilian—liked it very much." [Meyers, 296]

After the ten-day event ended, Lesley persuaded her father to visit Peru. There he enjoyed a visit to some Inca ruins, but his favorite part of the journey was the plane ride home. "I saw the wild parts of Brazil," he said, "that I'd never dreamed of seeing. You see unbroken wilderness." [Meyers, 296]

Honors continued to pour in. In 1955, Frost received an unprecedented second honorary degree from Dartmouth. John Sloan Dickey recalled that Frost's attitude toward these recognitions was "more bemused than anything. He enjoyed it, of course. He seemed genuinely to like public occasions. But he was a solitary man at heart. The honors, as he knew, were nothing beside the poems. The poems were everything. In that sense, he was the complete poet." [Parini, 395]

But two honors eluded Frost. He began suggesting indirectly that it would be a fine thing to receive honorary degrees from both Oxford and Cambridge. The only Americans to be paid this tribute in the past had been Henry Wadsworth Longfellow and James Russell Lowell, both in the 19th century. Frost carefully followed his own advice while making these overtures. "Sneak up on things," he once told an interviewer. "And never be caught looking as if you wanted them." [Meyers, 301]

In spite of public acclaim, Frost continued to wrestle with depression. In 1955, Ted and Kay Morrison's only son was killed in a car accident. The tragedy put the poet in the unusual position of setting aside his own feelings to comfort Kay rather than expecting encouragement from her. He also suffered from Irma's ongoing hospitalization and his uncertain relationship with Lesley. "He was himself struggling with many demons—family problems, unresolved," a friend observed. "He thought of the universe as a dark place with intermittent gleams of light." [Parini, 395] Much of his pain he kept to himself. "Every human being must learn to carry his own craziness and confusion and not bother his friends about it," he wrote in one of his notebooks. [Parini, 395–396]

As he had for most of his life, Frost drew on public commitments to fight his private demons. In December 1956, he received an invitation from the State Department to attend a London exhibit focused on his life and work, to be shown at the U.S. Embassy the following spring. The government thought that Frost, especially after his stellar performance in Brazil, would make an ideal goodwill ambassador to Britain at a time when, because of conflicting policy toward Egypt, relations between the two countries were strained.

Frost was attracted by the idea, but he was 82 years old. While enjoying better health than he'd had in years, he had a hearing loss that sometimes embarrassed him in public, and he was always susceptible to lung problems. He didn't want to travel to England simply to appear at an exhibition. In a letter to the State Department, he insisted, "If my country believes I can be of any use, even at my age, in reminding the British people of our own warm affection and strong friendship, why, of course, I'll go. I don't want to be an unguided missile, however; don't spare me. Tell me where you want me to go and when. I'll be ready." [Meyers, 301] Working with Kay, he renewed his indirect inquiries about receiving honorary degrees from Oxford and Cambridge. Letters inviting him to accept those awards arrived in March 1957. Replying to Oxford, Frost stated, "Few things could give me the pleasure of such an honor from the country ('half my own') that published my very first book. That was nearly fifty years ago when I was living and writing not fifty miles down the line from you in Beaconsfield. I shall look at it as a rounding out that we seldom get except in story books and none too often there." [Parini, 397]

On May 17, 1957, Robert Frost flew to London, planning to spend a month in England and Ireland. Just before he left, he wrote to the president of Amherst College, explaining why he couldn't attend the meeting of the college trustees. In his note, Frost alluded to the last lines of the Richard Lovelace's 17th-century poem "To Lucasta, Going to the Wars": "I may well say to my college after Lovelace: 'I could not love thee, dear, so much / Loved I not Honor more.'" [Meyers, 301]

AGES HENCE

Robert Frost's trip to England and Ireland in 1957 followed a breathtaking pace. His granddaughter Lesley Lee Francis, who accompanied him, later observed, "My grandfather thought this was his final journey, his last hurrah. He had put so much into it—one State Department official told me that few younger men could have sustained that schedule." [Parini, 404]

The poet received several honorary degrees. The presentations for the degrees from Oxford and Cambridge were made in Latin. Translated, the Oxford oration read, "Amid the clash of arms and mounting terror of our new instruments of war, [Frost's] poetry, with its echoes of Virgilian serenity, has brought, and will continue to bring, unfailing consolation to a suffering world." [Meyers, 303] The citation from Cambridge identified his ability to appeal to a wide range of readers: "His work is as pleasing to learned readers on account of the keen insight of his genius as it is, on account of its simplicity, to unschooled readers who become mired in the labyrinthine ambiguities of modern poets." [Meyers, 303–304]

Frost visited with old friends, including John Haines, whom he had not seen for almost 30 years. "My grandfather was obviously very moved by this visit," Lesley Lee Francis observed. "The friendship with Haines meant a good deal to him. They had never lost touch." [Parini, 400] Frost also visited Oldfields, where Edward Thomas had lived. Overcome with emotion as he thought of his friend who had been killed in World War I, Frost said, "There is no need to go inside." Instead he walked to the nearby orchard where the two men had spent many hours together, and after 10 minutes, walked silently back to his car.

The poet's schedule was peppered with official luncheons and dinners, as well as meetings with British poets and novelists, including Stephen Spender, Graham Greene, E.M. Forster, Edwin Muir, Cecil Day Lewis, and W.H. Auden. Several times, Frost encountered T.S. Eliot. During one visit, Eliot brought up the subject of Ezra Pound, who was still confined at St. Elizabeth's Hospital. Frost and Eliot's last meeting took place on June 11 at a formal dinner given for Frost. Eliot toasted his counterpart as "perhaps *the* most eminent, the most distinguished, I must call it, Anglo-American poet now living." Frost replied, "There's nobody living in either country I'd rather hear that from." [Meyers, 307]

As Frost flew home on June 20, he called the trip "a great experience— one of my greatest—more than that. Probably, all things considered, it *was* the greatest experience of my whole life." [Meyers, 308] About the only disappointment, aside from a brief illness, came from Frost's official biographer of more than 20 years, Lawrence Thompson, who traveled with the poet. The man infuriated Frost because, as he stated in a letter to Kay Morrison, "he began to criticize me and tell me what I ought to do next". [Meyers, 302] Over the years, Thompson had developed a great hostility toward Frost, and he no longer tried to hide those feelings. Eventually that anger caused Thompson to put the worst possible interpretation on events he recorded in his three-volume Frost biography.

Upon his return to the United States, Frost took up the cause of Ezra Pound. Frost did not like Pound and was deeply offended by Pound's actions during World War II; but he had also visited family members in insane asylums and told Louis Untermeyer that he "just couldn't stand the thought of any poet dying among a lot of drooling, obscene idiots." [Meyers, 311]

American writer Ernest Hemingway, who had been championing Pound's cause since the end of the war, wrote to Frost: "I detest Pound's politics, his antisemitism and his race-ism. But I truly feel it would do more harm to our country for Pound to die in confinement, than for him to be freed and sent to live with his daughter in Italy." [Meyers, 312–313]

Over the next several months, Frost paid three formal calls on U.S. Deputy Attorney General William Rogers to plead Pound's case. Finally in April 1958, Pound was released. American poet Archibald MacLeish, who also worked on Pound's behalf, recognized Frost's role. "Frost gets a large part of the credit," he wrote to Hemingway. "The old boy despises Ez for personal reasons but once he got started nothing could stop him and I think Rogers finally gave up out of sheer exhaustion." [Meyers, 315] Pound himself was less charitable. "He ain't been in much of a hurry," he stated when told of Frost's intervention. [Meyers, 315] As he boarded an Italian liner bound for Genoa, Pound gave the fascist salute.

Over the next three years, Frost fell into a pattern of spending summers in Vermont, occasionally appearing at Bread Loaf Writers' Conference, then briefly visiting Amherst. He stayed at his home in Cambridge during the early winter and celebrated Christmas with his friend Hyde Cox on an island off the Massachusetts coast. Soon after New Year's Day, he traveled to Florida, where Kay Morrison often visited. By early April, he had usually returned to Cambridge, and within a couple months had made his way back to Vermont.

Increasingly, however, Frost encountered physical problems, sometimes requiring hospitalization. While such incidents interfered with his public life, the old poet continued to give readings and lectures. His fame reached new heights because of his appearance at John F. Kennedy's presidential inauguration in January 1961. When Representative Stewart Udall of Arizona first suggested that Frost be invited to read at the event, Kennedy reportedly said, "Oh, no. You know that Robert Frost always steals any show he is part of." [Meyers, 322] While witnesses to the conversation differed in their view of whether Kennedy was joking, eventually the request was made, and Frost accepted.

Nearing 87 years old when President Kennedy took office, Robert Frost continued his involvement in goodwill missions for the U.S. government. In March and April of 1961, he traveled to Israel and Greece, places that fascinated him because of their historic importance. Unfortunately, he experienced a severe intestinal disorder while traveling. A British doctor who examined Frost at a stopover in England during his flight home said: "I can tighten up his bowels, all right, but it's his heart that worries me." [Parini, 419]

A weak heart would not slow the poet. After a brief rest in Cambridge, Frost returned to his regular schedule, while putting the finishing touches on his last book, *In the Clearing*. Published in the spring of 1962, the book contains many pieces of light verse, but also such notable poems as "Pod of the Milkweed" and "The Draft Horse". *In the Clearing* appeared 49 years after the publication of Frost's first book, *A Boy's Will*—a remarkably long career for a poet. "[Frost's] claim to distinction," observed critic W.W. Robson, "is the impressive level maintained in a large body of work." [Meyers, 329]

That spring President Kennedy presented Frost with the Congressional Gold Medal, originally awarded by President Eisenhower. A couple months later, the president asked Frost to travel to the Soviet Union as part of a cultural exchange. Although memories of health problems during his last overseas trip remained vivid, Frost agreed, and the State Department made arrangements for him to leave in August. "It's a grand adventure, isn't it?" Frost said to his translator on the plane. "This going to Russia, I mean. Crazy, too. At my age going all the way over there just to show off." [Parini, 427]

His Soviet hosts described Frost as a "worker poet, a poet of labor." In Leningrad, he met with Anna Akhmatova, considered by many to be the greatest Russian poet of the 20th century. When she recited some of her poems in Russian, Frost was struck by their musical quality. After a few days of travel, the American poet began experiencing severe stomach cramps, but he refused to let his health prevent him from meeting Soviet Premier Nikita Khrushchev. Khrushchev and Frost discussed cultural and political issues for 90 minutes, and the American argued that East and West Berlin should be reunited, a proposal Khrushchev did not embrace. The meeting ended with the two men shaking hands and exchanging compliments.

That fall, Robert Frost learned he needed surgery because of a prostate condition. Before he entered the hospital, he traveled to speaking engagements in Washington, D.C., Ohio, Michigan, and Illinois, and then returned to Cambridge. On December 2, he read poetry at the Ford Hall Forum in Boston, but when he finished, he felt weak and dizzy. The 88-year-old man needed assistance to reach his car.

The next day, Frost entered the hospital, where he underwent prostate surgery. Doctors removed cancerous tissue from his prostate and bladder, and he focused on recovery. On December 23, a pulmonary embolism and heart attack almost killed him. These episodes were the beginning of a series of life-threatening crises.

Frost and his friends received a break from the bad news on January 5, 1963, when word arrived that Yale University was awarding him the Bollingen Prize for *In the Clearing*. This award, he asserted, gave him "one new reason to live." [Parini, 439] Even as he entertained visitors from his hospital bed, however, Robert Frost knew his journey through life was nearing an end.

On January 27, Ezra Pound's daughter arrived at the hospital to thank Frost for his earlier efforts to free her father. After she left, he dictated a letter to some old friends. It ended with the words, "If only I get well . . . I'll go deeper into life with you than I ever have before." [Parini, 440] It was not to be. Near midnight the next day, another blood clot reached his lungs. Frost lost consciousness and shortly thereafter died.

As news of the loss of an American icon spread around the world, tributes poured in. President Kennedy summed up much of the praise when he spoke at the October 26 dedication of the Robert Frost Library at Amherst College:

> Today this college and country honor a man whose contribution was not to our size but to our spirit; not to our political beliefs but to our insight; not to our self-esteem but to our self-comprehension. . . . If Robert Frost was much honored during his lifetime, it was because a good many preferred to ignore his darker truths. . . . He brought an unsparing instinct for reality to bear on the platitudes and pieties of society. His sense of the human tragedy fortified him against self-deception and easy consolation. [Meyers, 352–353]

Robert Frost's life was over, but the process of revealing the contradictory man behind the public image had only begun. Wrestling with depression and personal tragedy, he found deliverance in commitments to the larger world. A poet who needed solitude, he thrived on companionship. And while his poems were often judged simple and old-fashioned, further study reveals layers of complexity and profound insight that remain fresh and relevant in a new century.

Works Cited

Meyers, Jeffrey. *Robert Frost: A Biography*. New York: Houghton Mifflin, 1996.

Parini, Jay. *Robert Frost: A Life*. New York: Henry Holt, 1999.

Sergeant, Elizabeth Shepley. *Robert Frost: The Trial By Existence*. New York: Holt, Rinehart and Winston, 1960.

Thompson, Lawrance. *Robert Frost: The Years of Triumph, 1915–1938*. New York: Holt, Rinehart and Winston, 1970.

———. *Robert Frost: The Early Years, 1874–1915*. New York: Holt, Rinehart and Winston, 1966.

———. *Fire and Ice: The Art and Thought of Robert Frost*. New York: Russell & Russell, 1942.

Walsh, John Evangelist. *Into My Own: The English Years of Robert Frost*. New York: Grove Press, 1988.

THOMAS MARCH

The Poetry of Robert Frost and the Creative Genius of Everyday Life

In his 1954 essay "The Prerequisites," Robert Frost (1874–1963) writes that "[a] poem is best read in the light of all the other poems ever written."[1] In this statement, Frost demonstrates a clear understanding of the inevitable connections that exist between great poets. A poem comes into existence at the urging of its maker but also against the backdrop of a tradition that defines it—that has established criteria for the poetic, in terms of both sensibility and the mechanics of form. Born in the century of American Transcendentalism and its Romantic celebration of simplicity and the sublimity of nature, Frost stands as both a twentieth century link to that tradition and as the protagonist in a personal poetic struggle to establish a new perspective on that tradition's primary concerns. Think of twentieth century American poets, and Robert Frost almost certainly leaps to mind among the most prolific, influential, and popular. During his lifetime, Frost achieved a personal fame unique among living poets, a fame ordinarily limited to the few that the public imagination can tolerate in its increasingly cluttered purview. Several of his books of verse won a Pulitzer Prize: *New Hampshire: A Poem With Notes and Grace Notes; A Further Range; A Witness Tree;* and *Collected Poems.* Amy Lowell, an American poet and critic to whom Frost turned for support and favor early in his career,[2] called him "one of the most intuitive" poets of the day[3] and noted that "[h]e sees much, . . . both into the hearts of persons, and into the qualities of scenes."[4]

Frost's fame and public approval were, however, far from unanimous. Critic Malcolm Cowley once noted, in "The Case Against Mr. Frost," in spite of his admiration for Frost's poetry, that "[s]ome of the honors heaped on him are less poetic than political. . . . [and] [h]e is being praised too often and with too great vehemence by people who don't like poetry."[5] Amy Lowell also notes, in addition to her praise and on the basis of only his first few books, that "his canvas is exceedingly small, and no matter how wonderfully he paints upon it, he cannot attain to the position held by men with a wider range of vision."[6] This "smallness" is balanced by the quality and depth of the "seeing" that Lowell praises, however. Esteemed American critic Edmund Wilson, in his 1926 essay "The All-Star Literary Vaudeville" writes: "Robert Frost has a thin but authentic vein of poetic sensibility; but I find him excessively dull, and he certainly writes poor verse."[7] Wilson's complaint, damning even in its thin vein of faint praise, takes Frost to task for the narrowness of his poetic vision. Frost himself, in a December 1914 letter to Sidney Cox, might even open the door to such criticism of his lack of aesthetic sensibility when he writes: "You aren't influenced by that Beauty is Truth claptrap. In poetry and under emotion every word used is 'moved' a little or much—moved from its old place, heightened, made, made new."[8] Although he attempts here to distance himself from a Romantic, specifically Keatsian, notion of Beauty, Frost reveals in these comments a sense of the status of poetry and emotion as equally creative. Poetry (the realm of the artist as such) and emotion (the well to which all have equal access) are conceived here as sharing an *intensity* of creative impulse and quality. It is a short step from these sentiments to the celebration of the creativity of ordinary, everyday life that Frost struggles to manifest in many of his poems—something akin to the "Prometheanism" that George Bagby, in "The Promethean Frost," associates with Frost's work. As Harold Bloom writes in his introduction to this series, "we can better find the work in the person, than we can discover that banal entity, the person in the work." The story of Frost's great poems is one of the emergence of elegant moments in which the poet captures the artistic, creative nature of human experience.

This sentiment links Frost with Walt Whitman—the poet of the previous century who found greatness in the ordinary. Yvor Winters has called Frost "an Emersonian Romantic"[9] and, less strongly, "something of an Emersonian."[10] And Frost shares the familiar venues, walks the familiar paths of the American Romantic tradition while distancing himself meaningfully from one of its great progenitors. Cowley spends much of "The Case Against Mr. Frost" challenging popular conceptions that compare Frost to those great poets and hail him as a representative poet of New Hampshire. In any event, poet and critic Robert Lowell tells us, in "Robert Frost: 1874–1963," that "[t]he thinker and poet that most influenced him was Emerson."[11] He goes on to explain that "[b]oth had something of the same highly urbane yet homemade finish and something of the same knack for verbal discovery."[12] Frost's own consciousness of his relation to Emerson is far from uncomplicated, however. Writing in his essay "On Emerson" Frost expresses some dissatisfaction with the Ralph Waldo Emerson he has come to know: "There is such a thing as getting too transcended. There are limits. Let's not talk socialism."[13] Taking his criticism beyond the poetic, Frost asserts: "I am not quite satisfied with the easy way Emerson takes disloyalty."[14] These comments fail to hide the sympathies between the two men's points of view, sympathies that become clear in many of Frost's most accomplished poems. In his seminal essay "Nature," Emerson asserts a relationship between nature and the observer that will become a consistent concern in Frost's poetry. He states that "the power to produce this delight"—the "suggestion of an occult relation between man and the vegetable" that he refers to earlier in the essay—"does not reside in nature, but in man, or in a harmony of both."[15] It is this special relationship, and more precisely an *awareness* of it, that Frost addresses and reveals in many of his poems. Even when they themselves may not be aware of it, the characters who inhabit Frost's poems are caught in a moment of seeing and constructing their harmony with nature. It is not always a harmony that resides in the celebration of nature for its own sake but, rather, in the display of his own and others' processes of constructing and contemplating the world around them, of coming to an understanding of significance—of the world, of the field, of the moment—and their place in relation to it. Frost strikes a balance between humility in the face of Nature and the elevation or celebration of the creative, artistic potential of the ordinary.

Of the poems in Frost's first collection, *A Boy's Will* (1913), "Mowing" stands apart. Frost himself was apparently of the same opinion, writing to Sidney Cox in December 1914: "I guess there is no doubt that is the best poem in Book I."[16] Frost's backward glance lands a few generations past his immediate precursors to re-imagine the mower and the scene of mowing, a particular favorite of Andrew Marvell's. Frost imagines this account of mowing in the mower's own words, from the mower's own perspective. And, indeed, this sonnet is less an account of the work of mowing itself, or of the individual's position as reaper among the plenty and bounty of what nature provides, than of the significance of one particular mower's *reflections* on that position. The mower inaugurates the poem by telling us that the only sound he notices as he works is that of his "long scythe whispering to the ground". (2) It immediately becomes clear, in the next line, that it's not the work that the scythe accomplishes but the process itself that has captured the attention of the mower. "What was it it whispered?" he asks, immediately answering, "I knew not well myself." (3) The mystery that the mower recognizes and with which he struggles for the remainder of the poem is one regarding the relations of things, the blade to that which it cuts and, by extension, the mower to the process itself.

It is a creative moment, one in which the mower contemplates and constructs a personal significance in and of the world around him. The mower abandons questions of how he has come to this moment—whether instigated by the "heat of the sun" (4) or merely by the negative possibilities produced by the general "lack of sound" (5). In his attempt to construct a significance for the sound of the scythe and his moment of awareness, he likewise rejects two easy but unsatisfying possibilities. Making sense of the sudden awareness of the scythe's sound is to be an opportunity for dreams neither of finished work, "no dream of the gift of idle hours" (7), nor of magically granted riches, "easy gold at the hand of fay or elf." (8) The mower seeks the truth, and rejects the fantasies to which the scythe's sound might lead in order to endow that sound with a significance that honors the wonder of the work itself. He affirms that "[a]nything more than the truth would have seemed too weak/to the earnest love that laid the swale in rows." (9–10)

The poet does not seek to exhaust the possibilities of the moment and its questions. The poem does not end on a note of neat completion, and the mower rejects the possibility that the scythe's message might signify triumph over the demands of work. Rather, the achievement of the mower, here, is to fully realize the significance of the moment's primary question about his own position in this landscape:

> The fact is the sweetest dream that labor knows.
> My long scythe whispered and left the hay to make. (14)

The mower ends by understanding that to have an answer, to be comforted by certainty, is a fantasy, "the sweetest dream". His ruminations end where they began, in an awareness of the whispering of the mower's tool, an ongoing satisfaction in work as opposed to dreams of its cessation. Frost frames the mower's moment of noticing as an opportunity to come to understanding by means of reflection. It is also a moment of choice between facile dreams of ease and the more difficult rejection of such dreams in favor of an appreciation of the mystery of the moment and the speculation it engenders.

How does Frost conceive of poetry as a vehicle through which one may examine, even celebrate, the creative impetus reflected in the contemplation of the moment and in the encounter of a mind with nature in even its smallest forms? The question is not, entirely, a poetic one, although Frost certainly has a great deal to say about poetics in his letters and other prose work. Moments in Frost's prose provide some insight into how a focus on the moment enables the poet to create a frame that accentuates the very process of framing and creating significance or meaning in the world. This answers, in part, the question of form—for poetry is uniquely amenable to the examination of the moment, not in its potential for brevity but rather in its intensity of language and circumstance, in its ability to simultaneously delineate and expand upon the moment. In his essay, "The Figure a Poem Makes," Frost writes of the poem that:

> It begins in delight and ends in wisdom. . . . It begins in delight, it inclines to the impulse, it assumes direction with the first line laid down, it runs a course of lucky events, and ends in a clarification of life—not necessarily a great clarification such as sects and cults are founded on, but in a momentary stay against confusion.[17]

The "clarification of life" that Frost alludes to here is apparent in "Mowing"; Frost's characterization of this clarification as a "momentary stay against confusion" reminds us, as that poem does, that the delights of discovery, of noticing something and taking the time to consider it, need not end ultimately in perfect knowledge or even any knowledge at all. This kind of clarification begins in the question posed by noticing, by becoming aware, and may often end there as well.

In many of his poems, Frost provides settings in which this clarifying moment comes to the forefront. The exploration of such moments, as they are lingered in and upon, demonstrates that the search for clarification—or, rather, the emergence of its possibility in the moment observed—is itself inherently creative. In his famous 1935 letter to *The Amherst Student*, Frost writes:

> There is at least so much good in the world that it admits of form and the making of form. . . . In us nature reaches its height of form and through us exceeds itself. . . . The artist, the poet, might be expected to be the most aware of such assurance, but it is really everybody's sanity to feel it and live by it.[18]

Form exists not simply in the acts of selection, arrangement, and emphasis that characterize poetic production but in the everyday acts of seeking and creating clarity that may go unnoticed but comprise our understanding of the world. Frost continually strives to achieve a poetic form that is amenable to the examination of how this kind of form itself comes to be. Such moments, for Frost, are not simply worthy of poetic attention but worthy of consideration as poetic in themselves.

Similarly, in a letter to Kimball Flaccus, Frost notes that poetry "should be of major adventures only, outward or inward—important things that happen to you, or important things that occur to you. Mere poeticality won't suffice."[19] (111) Frost himself might not always meet this criterion of subordinating "mere poeticality" to the importance of the occurrence itself. However, the proof of this commitment lies not in the letters or Frost's other public ruminations on writing. The prose stands as a testament to Frost's self-conscious writerly struggles with questions of significance and emphasis. The proof lies in the poems. And throughout Frost's career, the best of the poems, just a few of which we'll examine here, celebrate the importance of the thought, of glimpses of realization in the moment of occurrence or in memory. From Frost's first book, *A Boy's Will* (1913), through the subsequent major collections—which include *North of Boston* (1914); *Mountain Interval* (1916); *New Hampshire* (1923);*West-Running Brook* (1928); *Collected Poems* (1930; 1939); *A Further Range* (1936); *A Witness Tree* (1942); *Steeple Bush* (1947); and *In the Clearing* (1962)—a concern for creating a poetic framework for the meditative moment appears consistently, in the lesser-known poems as well as in some of his most famous.

Amy Lowell praised the poet of "Mowing" and "Mending Wall" (among others), noting that "[t]his is not the work of a mere observer, but of a man who has lived what he writes about."[20] "Mending Wall," published in Frost's *North of Boston*, explores the possibilities of communion and the ultimate clash of interpretations that abound in a moment of shared labor. The unity—or at the very least, openness and trust—that the poet finds occasion to long for here is a motive that he ascribes likewise to nature: "Something there is," he tells us, "that doesn't love a wall." (1, 35) The first instance of this observation serves as the preliminary to the poet's establishment of the poem's scenario—two neighbors who find themselves undertaking the ritual chore of restoring the stones that have fallen from the wall that separates their properties. Prior even to his own direct questioning of the need for such a wall, the poet describes the wall's emerging gaps—the very things he has set out to repair—in almost mystical terms. They appear as if by magic: "No one has seen them made or heard them made, / But at spring mending-time we find them there." (10–11) Nature, it would seem, favors connection over this walling off of the land—an activity, Frost notes, that ironically encourages community and connection only by restoring the limiting and divisive function of the wall. As in "Mowing," Frost seizes an opportunity to portray an awakening to the significance of one's work beyond the physical act of labor itself.

In the act of rebuilding, the poet realizes that like the mysterious forces that refuse to allow the wall to remain whole, he neither needs nor understands the wall. When he tries to explain his position to his neighbor, observing that neither suffers from a threat of incursion by the other, the neighbor responds that "[g]ood fences make good neighbors." (33) In its first occurrence, the significance of this phrase seems straightforward enough. A good fence stands as a marker of boundaries that neighbors do not cross, uninvited, and thus ensures that neither party presumes upon the bounty or solitude of the other. This statement provokes the poet to further rumination, and he fantasizes about how he would like to question his neighbor about the purpose and value of walls. He concludes his imaginary monologue with a repetition of the observation that "[s]omething there is that doesn't love a wall." (35) With the poet's objections to walls firmly established, the phrase takes on new significance. Walls are not only physically unnatural, in the context of the poet's mystification of nature's urge toward decay, but symbolic of the very lack of understanding against which the poet is struggling. The demands of rebuilding don't stop in the face of his wondering "[w]hy . . . they make good neighbors" (30), but he lacks the comfort or familiarity required to pose the question aloud.

The statement "We keep the wall between us as we go" (15) begins as an observation of fact, but by the end of the poem it has acquired additional significance as a symbol of the poet's inability to make a meaningful connection with his neighbor. Indeed, the neighbor, who "moves in darkness," (40) is incapable, in the poet's estimation, of the kind of inquiry that the poet imagines might enable them to share more than a common barrier. "He will not," Frost notes, "go behind his father's saying," (43) taking for granted the truth of the aphorism with no apparent desire to test this truth beyond the weight of the stones he carries. When it first appears, the phrase functions as a starting point for the poet's own musings about the necessity of walls. Ending the poem with his neighbor's pleased and unquestioning repetition of the phrase—"He says again, 'Good fences make good neighbors'" (45)—Frost positions the statement in response to his own (silent) longing for his neighbor to "go behind" these words, and thus invites us to do so in the neighbor's stead. Reflecting, with Frost, as his neighbor has not been invited to do, we recall that the gaps in the wall stand—unmended—as opportunities to connect but also that, even in their mending, these fallen fences have required a coming together. This creates an *opportunity* in the actual making of good fences to lead to the creation of a "neighborly" relationship—even in the act of reinforcing a symbolic barrier. Frost lays bare the process of burgeoning awareness and creativity that this scene inspires in the mind of his protagonist. From this vantage point, it becomes clear that the poet's own timidity combined with the neighbor's stubbornness, has ensured that the only understanding achieved by the poet, for himself and for us, is about the tenacious inertia of separateness.

In what is perhaps his most famous poem, "The Road Not Taken," from *Mountain Interval*, Frost examines the richness of possibility contained in a moment of decision. In the first three of the poem's four stanzas the traveler meditates on the differences between two roads as he decides which he should follow. He is "sorry [he cannot] travel both." (2) That is, the *need* to choose is regrettable; Frost inaugurates the poem with these simple observations of opportunity and regret in order to establish a moment in which the traveler becomes aware of the consequences of choosing, that one set of possibilities must be left behind forever. His first response is to attempt to anticipate the future, determine what lies at the end of either road as he looked "down one as far as I could / To where it bent in the undergrowth." (4–5) The thought continues into the next stanza, as he makes a similar attempt with the second road, the one least worn. But anticipation is impossible, and the difference between the two roads ultimately lies not in what lies at the end of either road but in the second road's having "the better claim" (7) due to its being "grassy and want[ing] wear." (8) The second stanza ends, however, with an immediate correction, as though the poet has exaggerated this better claim and cannot avoid noticing that, to be fair, "the passing there / Had worn them really about the same." (9–10)

This notion of the roads' equivalence extends into the first two lines of the third stanza: "And both that morning equally lay / In leaves no step had trodden black." (11–12) The poet's prior consideration of the roads' general quality yields here to a realization that the roads are equally fresh and inviting at this particular moment. The decision to take the "grassy" road is actually arbitrary. We learn later that he has chosen to take "the one less traveled by" (19), but in the actual moment of choice, the poet does not indicate that this decision stems directly from the road's lack of wear. In fact, he informs us of his choice in a simple exclamation that follows his acknowledgement that the roads are equally appealing: "Oh, I kept the first for another day!" (13) This exclamation stands in contrast to the declarative quality of the rest of the poem, but it is as ambivalent as it is emphatic. There is certainly a sense of urgency here, suggesting that the decision was made hastily. But is this a cry of regret or pride?

In the poem's final stanza, Frost shifts the focus to a time when this moment of decision is a thing of the past and reinforces the ambivalence first apparent in his description of that decision. The "sigh" that signals the poet's moment of recollection can signify either regret or fondness for the memory. Similarly, after restating the initial dilemma of the two roads' divergent possibilities, Frost ends the poem with a statement about the significance of his decision: "I took the one less traveled by, / And that has made all the difference." (19–20) This significance, however, is stated in the simplest and most ambiguous of terms. The "difference" alluded to here is neither negative nor positive. The apparent rush to decide may have resolved the dilemma in the moment of its first occurrence. But Frost's narrator seeks to remind us not only that judgment has consequences, but also that small distinctions, in the moment of their discovery, can achieve significance that far outweighs their first appearance.

"Birches" from *Mountain Interval* begins with the immediate creative transfiguration of the birch trees. Although presented as one verse paragraph, the poem proceeds in its 59 lines through several iterations of the poet's observation of the birch tree and its significance. The poem begins with a simple statement of how the sight of birch trees provokes a particular fond musing:

> When I see birches bend to left and right
> Across the lines of straighter darker trees,
> I like to think some boy's been swinging them. (1–3)

The poet's preference seems arbitrary—why a boy, and why swinging? The questions provoked here will linger until the poet has rejected other interpretations of the scene that enter his imagination next. The poet speculates that a possible and alternative explanation of the birches' bending is the weight of ice on the branches during winter. Frost allows us access to the full extent of this association, as he ponders how such ice-laden birches "click upon themselves / . . . and turn many-colored" (7–8) and ultimately "shed crystal shells" (10) as the sun warms the ice away. This association is not without its beauty, certainly. And, indeed, Frost goes on to observe that, in the shower of these shells, "[y]ou'd think the inner dome of heaven had fallen." (13) In spite of the beauty of this explanation, the poet shifts away from these observations after line 20, returning to considerations of the birch tree's personal significance in his reflections.

The poet characterizes the image of the boy's playful influence on the trees as preferable to that of the ice storm and its beautiful ravages. As he turns back to the imaginary boy, Frost characterizes the intervening description as sterile, in spite of its beauty:

> But I was going to say when Truth broke in
> With all her matter of fact about the ice storm,
> I should prefer to have some boy bend them . . . (21–23)

Frost brushes away his earlier reverie as mere "fact," bound to the insolent demands of a distracting "Truth". The irony here is that even this realm of "fact" has come into being by means of the poet's own creative consciousness, that his *own* yielding to considerations of bare facts, independent of human intervention, has resulted nevertheless in the conveyance of a *sense* of an ice storm's ravages that transcends the mere fact of them. Indeed, Amy Lowell notes that we can see "by the description of the ice-covered birch trees, how eagerly he offered his mind to the impress of such pictures".[21] The image of the boy bending the branches in play is one of carefree merriment, of *finding* fun in the resources of one's own imagination. This boy, "too far from town to learn baseball" (25) learns to amuse himself with "what he found himself" (26) "and could play alone." (27) Solitude, far from pitiable, is both prelude to and instigator of resourcefulness; and the mind's resourcefulness is precisely what this poem both enacts and celebrates as it displays alternative considerations of the birches and their peculiar appearance. Frost demonstrates how the boy transforms the riding of birch tree branches from a game into an art in and of itself. The description of the boy's activities in learning to master the trees yields to a contemplation of his careful technique:

> . . . He always kept his poise
> To the top branches, climbing carefully
> With the same pains you use to fill a cup
> Up to the brim, and even above the brim.
> Then he flung outward, feet first, with a swish,
> Kicking his way down through the air to the ground.
> (35–37)

The boy's actions are careful as well as carefree; he has achieved a balance between caution and exuberance that not only ensures his safety but also demonstrates an expertise that can only arise from diligent experience.

Frost initiates the poem's final section with a recollection that associates his own position with that of the boy: "So was I once myself a swinger of birches. / And so I dream of going back to be." (41–42) Frost evinces a fond longing for this child's luxury of time and energy. As he confesses the comfort of this memory, Frost begins to establish a new significance for the birch trees:

> It's when I'm weary of considerations,
> And life is too much like a pathless wood (44–45)
> [. . .]

> I'd like to get away from earth awhile
> And then come back to it and begin over. (48–49)

The birch trees—in their individual beauty expressed earlier in the poem, and in the ease and luxury of solitude signified by the imaginary boy who ultimately stands in for the poet's memory of an earlier, carefree self—provided a comforting object upon which to meditate when the quotidian concerns of life become not only tiring but confusing. Birches carve a path through that "pathless wood" by connecting the poet to considerations of beauty and freedom that *do* matter, in the face of all else. Although they may appear to manifest simple regret, lines 48–49 contain a longing for the restoration of possibility. He does not desire the erasure of the past, however:

> May no fate willfully misunderstand me
> And half grant what I wish and snatch me away
> Not to return. Earth's the right place for love: (50–52)

The poet longs for the reemergence of the freedom of *temporary* escape that the birches provide for the boy. And such an escape means nothing without the promise of return. He wants to climb "*[t]oward* heaven" (56), his own emphasis calling attention to the limits of this desire; in such a moment, it's the direction that matters, not the achievement of either the life-ending goal of a metaphysical heaven or a whimsical physical escape into the sky, away from the earth (and the love it harbors). Indeed, this activity is to continue until the moment when "the tree could bear no more, / But dipped its top" (56–57) to return the poet back to earth.

This comfort of physical return reflects the comfort of return to memory and the recollection of moments of possibility that the first two considerations of the birches establish. Even the "Truth" that Frost appears almost to resent earlier in the poem is now a source of comfort, a truth that more fully emerges as a function of the poet's memory and consciousness. Frost accomplishes this definition of personal truth by compounding three frames of sense in the poem, in iterations of beauty and its various sources that stand not in opposition to each other but as equally viable considerations, each of which casts the others in relief. Similarly, in his essay "Above the Brim" poet and Nobel laureate Seamus Heaney praises the "airy vernal daring, an overbrimming of invention,"[22] among other things, that Frost manifests in this poem and elsewhere. The unique beauty of each moment of the poet's consideration stands alone, coming into being as though the poet were attempting and adjusting a new lens through which to view this scene. And from any of the birches' places—the world of the "matter of fact, the projected abstraction of the imaginary boy, the poet's own memory and ultimate comfort—the poet can proceed, or return, to another. "One could do worse," the poet wryly comments in the poem's final line, "than be a swinger of birches." (59) One could, instead, fall prey to a different, destructive swinging of an entirely different sort, between subjugating the self to the weariness of the quotidian and a complete and final escape that offers no promise of a refreshing return.

In another of his most well-known poems, *New Hampshire*'s "Stopping by Woods on a Snowy Evening," Frost meditates on the desire to pause and explore the woods—and the responsibilities that can interfere with the fulfillment of that desire. In the poem's first stanza, Frost's description of his surroundings serves to establish the desire to linger and also to underscore the privacy of the moment. Frost begins in the first stanza by identifying the probable ownership of the woods he has just encountered. What is important here is not the fact that the poet may know whose property he contemplates invading, but that the person is away. As a consequence, "He will not see me stopping here / To watch his woods fill up with snow." (3–4) The desire is clearly to linger in this place for some time, calmly contemplating the falling snow—for woods do not fill with snow in a few minutes.

In the second and third stanzas, Frost continues to reinforce the privacy of the scene. He first deflects attention from his own desires by observing the behavior of his horse: "My little horse must think it queer / To stop without a farmhouse near." (5–6) This description of the horse's thinking establishes the strangeness of the scene; stopping without a landmark to signal the journey's end is a puzzling experience for the horse. Clearly, this is an irregular moment, a delay in the journey. Frost reinforces this sense of irregularity in the first lines of the third stanza with a description of the horse's agitation: "He gives his harness bells a shake / To ask if there is some mistake." (9–10) The horse's presence, here and in the second stanza, reminds us of the original purpose of the journey and provides the poet with a way to change that purpose. As long as he ignores the horse, and the fulfillment of the obligation toward which his horse would carry him, he can enjoy the promise of the scene that surrounds him.

Each description of the horse is followed by the poet's return to a description of the surroundings. In the third stanza, the poet provides greater detail about his position: "Between the woods and frozen lake / The darkest evening of the year." (7–8) He begins to make more of his surroundings, and he also indicates the uniqueness of this particular night. Its status as "the darkest evening" can be significant in a number of ways. If purely denotative, this reference to darkness signifies the possibility of maximum privacy and decreased risk of detection or interruption. This darkness may also signify the night's *duration*; in this context, the poet is speculating about the amount of *time* he could spend lingering in contemplation and exploration. In the fourth stanza, the sound of the horse's bells conveying impatience and confusion reminds us that a larger goal has been temporarily delayed for whatever is happening in this moment. The poet then turns from the sound of the bells to the other sounds in his environment:

> The only other sound's the sweep
> Of easy wind and downy flake. (11–12)

These lines clarify the poet's attraction to this scene. In contrast to the tasks of the poet's horse-and-buggy journey—and the length and importance of the journey remain undisclosed—this moment of stopping by the woods is a scene of comfort and softness.

In the final stanza, the poet succumbs to the message delivered by the harness bells and carries on with his journey, rejecting the invitation to linger because he has "promises to keep." (14) The previous stanzas have served a dual purpose—that of providing time for the poet to fully realize and express his desire for privacy and time to respond to the opportunities that have arisen, while at the same time deferring the inevitable need to fulfill his mission. Finally, we learn just what it is that the poet sees in these woods: "The woods are lovely, dark, and deep." (13) Malcolm Cowley suggests that woods, in Frost's poetry, "seem to be his symbol for the uncharted country within ourselves, full of possible beauty, but also full of horror."[23] And here the woods clearly invite exploration and further reflection on their beauty. But the poet does not possess the luxury of time that would allow for either. The repetition in the final two lines—"And miles to go before I sleep, / And miles to go before I sleep" (15–16)—brings the intensity of the poet's desire to stay into greater focus. The final stanza is also marked by a change in the rhyme scheme—AABA BBCB CCDC—that Frost has established in the first three stanzas. The lines of stanza four rhyme consistently—DDDD—further emphasizing the monotony of the journey ahead, which promises exhaustion. The journey's purpose is the mere fulfillment of "promises," obligations that take the poet away from the solitude and reflective time he so desires and back into realm of personal relationships and their demands.

Frost's celebration of the creative quality of experience extends as far as "In Winter in the Woods. . .," the final poem of his final collection, *In the Clearing*. The poem is a simple narrative in three stanzas, telling the story of the poet's foray into the woods to cut down a maple tree. The first line—"In the winter in the woods alone"—establishes the solitude of the scene but also functions to acknowledge the sensibility that has characterized Frost's career from the beginning. This is especially apparent in the third line, "I mark a maple for my own"; Frost's work has consistently been characterized by such figurative acts of marking. Here, however, he has marked the maple so that he may cut it down. The second stanza seems at first to serve merely a transitional function, to get the poet out of the woods and into the present moment of reflection on this event. After felling the tree, the poet moves out of the woods, leaving behind "a line of shadowy tracks / Across the tinted snow." (7–8) He has left his mark, not only in the felled tree, but also in the tracks that remain as evidence of his presence. The first two stanzas attempt to establish a range of possible significance for this moment of encounter with the woods. The poet selects and chops down, from all of the trees in the forest, the one tree that meets his needs. The absence of the tree remains as an indelible marker of his presence. But as he retreats, he leaves a mark that reflects the ephemeral nature of this presence: footprints in the snow that will not last as a testament to his effect on these woods.

In the final stanza, which could stand as a poem in its own right, the poet arrives at a new understanding:

> I see for Nature no defeat
> In one tree's overthrow
> Or for myself in my retreat
> For yet another blow. (9–12)

Set apart, these lines reflect the shared resilience of the woods and the poet. As a statement on the activities that make up the previous two stanzas of the poem, these lines retain this significance and gain another. At the scene of chopping, and in the scene of retreat, the poet has already provided a sense of how he experiences these moments as opportunities to exert his will as well as to mark his presence. In the poem's final four lines, the poet makes a new judgment on these activities in the moment of reflection that occurs after his retreat from the woods. The judgment attempts to justify the act of felling the tree—nature won't be "defeated" by the loss of one of its trees— and also an assertion of personal resilience that defies the anonymity of the stump and the ephemeral footprints. *He* will not be defeated. The "blow" to come promises not only a return but the retention of the memory of his deeds and the importance of what and how he has observed in these moments. In this final poem of his final collection, Frost succinctly establishes the ironic presence of creativity within a moment of destruction.

Reflecting on the significance of Frost's work, Robert Lowell writes: "I used to wonder if I knew anything about the country that wasn't in Frost. I always had the pleasure of either having my knowledge confirmed or learning something new that completed it."[24] Lowell invokes a relation between art and life that Oscar Wilde formulates in his dialogue "The Decay of Lying" from *Intentions*. Speaking through the character Vivian, Wilde asserts: "Life imitates art far more than Art imitates life."[25] (307) For Lowell, the life that is the country and his *experience* of the country have been irrevocably shaped by Frost's art. Wilde also observes that "[i]f. . . we regard Nature as the collection of phenomena external to man, people only discover in her what they bring to her."[26] (301) According to Wilde, people bring, consciously or unconsciously, a set of expectations about life that art has cultivated and placed in them.

The activity Wilde describes—bringing expectations to every encounter in life—is itself an artistic act. It is this insight that Frost's poetry captures, when the circumstances of the poems involve an encounter with nature and also when they do not. Yvor Winters has commented that some of the perspectives manifested in Frost's poetry "effectually cut Frost off from any really profound understanding of human experience, whether political, moral, metaphysical, or religious."[27] But the poems, at their best, do demonstrate that experience—in action and in the otherwise silent and invisible action of thought—is art, that there is a common denominator of creativity that infuses all of our moments of noticing, regardless of whether we are actively conscious of this fact. In the world of Frost's poetry such creation is not the domain only of those artists who are lucky enough to know themselves as such. As Frost muses in a July 1913 letter to F.S. Flint, written at the beginning of his career: "I am no propagandist of equality. But I enjoy above all things the contemplation of equality where it happily exists."[28]

NOTES

1.   Reprinted in Elaine Barry, ed. *Robert Frost on Writing*. New Brunswick: Rutgers University Press, 1973, 139.
2.   Barry, 150.
3.   A. Lowell, 80.
4.   A. Lowell, 127.
5.   Cowley, 37.
6.   A. Lowell, 135.
7.   Wilson, "The All-Star Literary Vaudeville," *The Shores of Light: A Literary Chronicle of the Twenties and Thirties*. New York: Farrar, Straus, & Young, 1952.
8.   Reprinted in Barry, ed., 68.
9.   Winters, 58.

10. Winters, 60.

11. Lowell, Robert. "Robert Frost: 1874-1963," *Selections: From the First Two Issues of* The New York Review of Books. Ed. Robert B. Silvers and Barbara Epstein. NY: The New York Review of Books, n.d. (reprint), 75.

12. Ibid.

13. Reprinted in Cox and Lathem, eds., 115.

14. Ibid., 117–18.

15. Emerson, Ralph Waldo. "Nature," *Selections from Ralph Waldo Emerson: An Organic Anthology*. Ed. Stephen E. Whicher. Boston: Riverside Editions—Houghton Mifflin Co., 1960, 24.

16. From "To Sidney Cox" in Elaine Barry, ed. *Robert Frost on Writing*. New Brunswick: Rutgers University Press, 1973, 68.

17. Reprinted in Barry, ed., 126.

18. Reprinted in Barry, ed., 113.

19. Reprinted in Barry, ed., 111.

20. A. Lowell, 92.

21. A. Lowell, 88.

22. Heaney, 74.

23. Cowley 43.

24. R. Lowell, 76.

25. Wilde, 307.

26. Wilde, 301.

27. Winters, 75.

28. Reprinted in Barry, ed., 83.

MALCOLM COWLEY

The Case Against Mr. Frost

Robert Frost has been heaped with more official and academic honors than any other American poet, living or dead. Although he was never graduated from college, having left Dartmouth after two months and Harvard after two years (and more credit to his dogged independence), he holds by the last count seventeen honorary degrees. He was twice made a Master of Arts (by Amherst and Michigan), three times a Doctor of the Humanities (by Vermont, Wesleyan and St. Lawrence) and twelve times a Doctor of Letters (by Yale, Middlebury, Bowdoin, New Hampshire, Columbia, Williams, Dartmouth, Bates, Pennsylvania, Harvard, Colorado and Princeton). He has been chosen a Phi Beta Kappa poet by Tufts, William and Mary, Harvard (twice) and Columbia. He has been a professor at Amherst; a poet in residence and a fellow in letters at Michigan; a Charles Eliot Norton professor, a Ralph Waldo Emerson fellow and a fellow in American civilization at Harvard, all these being fairly lucrative appointments. He has been awarded four Pulitzer Prizes, one more than E. A. Robinson and two more than Stephen Vincent Benét, the only other poets to be named more than once. He has also received the Loines Prize for poetry, the Mark Twain medal, the gold medal of the National Institute of Arts and Letters and the silver medal of the Poetry Society of America. His work has been the subject of at least two full-length critical studies, many brochures, pamphlets, bibliographies and a memorial volume, *Recognition of Robert Frost*, not to

Malcolm Cowley, "The Case Against Mr. Frost," *The New Republic* (September 11, 1944), pp. 312–313; (September 18, 1944), pp. 345–47. Reprinted by permission of the author and The New Republic.

mention hundreds of essays which, some discordant notes in the early years, have ended as a vast diapason of praise.

And Frost deserves all these honors, both for his poetry in itself and for a long career devoted to the art of verse. In a country where poets go to seed, he has kept his talent ready to produce perfect blossoms (together with some that are misshapen or overgrown). It is a pleasure to name over the poems of his youth and age that become more vivid in one's memory with each new reading: the dramatic dialogues like "The Death of the Hired Man" and "The Witch of Coös," besides half a dozen others almost equally good; the descriptions or narrations that turn imperceptibly into Aesop's fables, like "The Grindstone" and "Cow in Apple Time"; and, best of all, the short lyrics like "The Pasture," "Now Close the Windows," "The Sound of the Trees," "Fire and Ice," "Stopping by the Woods on a Snowy Evening" (always a favorite with anthologists), "To Earthward," "Tree at My Window," "Acquainted with the Night," "Neither out Far Nor in Deep," "Beech," "Willful Homing," "Come In" . . . and I could easily add to the list. One of his best lyrics was written in 1892; when Frost was a freshman at Dartmouth; three or four others were included in his latest book, *A Witness Tree*, published just fifty years later; and these recent poems show more skill and density of expression than almost anything he had written before. This same volume and the one that preceded it—*A Further Range*, published in 1936— also contain bad poems that have been almost equally admired: long monologues in pedestrian blank verse, spoken as if from a cracker barrel among the clouds, and doggerel anecdotes directed (or rather, indirected) against the New Deal; but a poet has the right to be judged by his best work, and Frost at his best has added to our little store of authentic poetry.

If in spite of this I still say that there is a case against him and room for a dissenting opinion, perhaps I chiefly mean that there is a case against the zealous admirers who are not content to take the poet for what he is, but insist on using him as a sort of banner for their own moral or political crusades.

We have lately been watching the growth in this country of a narrow nationalism that has spread from politics into literature (although its literary adherents are usually not political isolationists). They demand, however, that American literature should be affirmative, optimistic, uncritical and "truly of this nation." They have been looking round for a poet to exalt; and Frost, through no fault of his own (but chiefly through the weaker qualities of his work), has been adopted as their symbol. Some of the honors heaped on him are less poetic than political. He is being praised too often and with too great vehemence by people who don't like poetry. And the result is that his honors shed very little of their luster on other poets, who in turn feel none of the pride in his achievements that a battalion feels, for example, when one of its officers is cited for outstanding services. Instead Frost is depicted by his admirers as a sort of Sunday-school paragon, a saint among miserable sinners. His common sense and strict Americanism are used as an excuse for berating and belittling other poets, who have supposedly fallen into the sins of pessimism, obscurity, obscenity and yielding to foreign influences; we even hear of their treachery to the American dream. Frost, on the other hand, is depicted as loyal, autochthonous and almost aboriginal. We are told not only that he is "the purest classical poet of America today"—and there is some truth in Gorham B. Munson's early judgment—but also that he is "the one great American poet of our time" and "the only living New Englander in the great tradition, fit to be placed beside Emerson, Hawthorne and Thoreau."

But when Frost is so placed and measured, his stature seems greatly diminished; it is almost as if a tough little Morgan horse, the best of its breed, had been judged by the standards that apply to Clydesdales and Percherons. Height, breadth and strength: he falls short in all these qualities of the great New Englanders. And the other quality for which he is often praised, his utter faithfulness to the New England spirit, is not one of the virtues they knowingly cultivated. They realized that the New England spirit, when it stands alone, is inclined to be narrow and arithmetical. It has reached its finest growth only when cross-fertilized with alien philosophies.

Hinduism, Sufism, Fourierism and German Romanticism: each of these doctrines contributed its own share to the New England renaissance of the 1850's. Even Thoreau, who died almost in sight of his birthplace, said that he had traveled much in Concord; he spoke of bathing his intellect "in the stupendous and cosmogonal philosophy of the Bhagvat-Geeta. . . . The pure Walden water," he said, "is mingled with the sacred water of the Ganges." And Hawthorne, who told us that "New England is quite as large a lump of earth as my heart can really take in," was eager for any new ideas that might help to explain the nature of New Englanders as individuals or as members of society. The books he borrowed from the Salem Athenaeum during the ten lonely years he spent at home included the complete works, in French, of Rousseau, Voltaire (several times), Pascal, Racine (several times) and the "Essais" of Montaigne, as well as a great number of volumes on science, philosophy, general history and the past of New England.1 Some of his weaker contemporaries were quite unbalanced by the foreign learning with which they overloaded their minds; but the stronger ones assimilated everything and, in the end, reasserted their own New England natures, which had become immensely richer.

And even Frost, as purely Yankee as his character seems today, was partly formed by his three years abroad. The turning point in his life was when he sold his first New Hampshire farm (which his grandfather had bought for him on condition that he live there at least ten years) and when, in 1912, his wife said, "Let's go to England and live under thatch." In England he made the reputation that enabled him to continue his career as a poet (and also as a "poet in residence"). In England, too, he had the experience of meeting other poets who understood what he was trying to say: Lascelles Abercrombie, Rupert Brooke, Wilfred Wilson Gibson and Edward Thomas. They were willing to learn from him, and Frost, in a sense, learned even more from them: that is, he learned to abandon the conventional language of the Late Victorians and to use his own speech without embarrassment. It is interesting to compare *A Boy's Will*, published in London but written in New Hampshire before his English journey, with "Mountain Interval," published after his return to this country in 1915 but written chiefly in England. The poems in *A Boy's Will* gave his own picture of the world, but in the language of the genteel poets; they were full of "maidens pale," "sweet pangs" and "airy dalliance." The poems written in the English countryside used the language that is spoken north of Boston. Once it had been regarded as a mere dialect only to be used in ballads like "Skipper Ireson's Ride" and in satirical comments like "The Biglow Papers"; but Frost in England had done what Hemingway would later do in Paris: he had raised his own idiom to the dignity of a literary language.

It was after his return that he carried the process further. Having learned to write New Hampshire, he also began to think New Hampshire, in the sense of accepting its older customs as immutable laws. . . .

II

In spite of his achievements as a narrative and lyric poet . . . there is a case against Robert Frost as a social philosopher in verse and as a representative of the New England tradition. He is too much walled in by the past. Unlike the great Yankees of an earlier age, he is opposed to innovations in art, ethics, science, industry or politics. Thus, in one of his longer blank-verse monologues, he bridles when he hears a "New York alec" discussing Freudian psychology, which Frost dismisses as "the new school of the pseudo-phallic." Elsewhere he objects to researches in animal behavior (which he calls "instituting downward comparisons"), to new inventions (saying that ingenuity should be held in check) and even to the theory of evolution—or at least he ridicules one farmer who speaks of it admiringly, whereas he sympathizes with another who stops him on the road to say:

The trouble with the Mid-Victorians
Seems to have been a man named John L. Darwin.

New ideas seem worse to him if they come from abroad, and worst, of all if they come from Russia. He is continually declaiming against the Russians of all categories: the pessimistic Russians, the revolutionary Russians, the collectivistic Russians, the five-year-planning Russians: he seems to embrace them all in a global and historical dislike that extends from Dostoevsky to Dnieperstroy. He is horrified by the thought that New England might be exposed to the possibility of adopting any good or bad feature of the Russian program. Thus, after reading about a project for rural rehabilitation, he hastened to write:

> It is in the news that all these pitiful kin
> Are to be bought out and mercifully gathered in
> To live in villages next to the theatre and store
> Where they won't have to think for themselves any more;
> While greedy good-doers, beneficent beasts of prey,
> Swarm over their lives, enforcing benefits
> That are calculated to soothe them out of their wits,
> And by teaching them how to sleep the sleep all day,
> Destroy their sleeping at night the ancient way.

Sometimes Frost decides that it would be a relief "To put these people at one stroke out of their pain"—these people being the marginal farmers; then next day he wonders how it would be if someone offered to put an end to his own troubles. The upshot is that he proposes to do nothing whatever, being satisfied with the New England countryside as it is—or rather, as it was in his early manhood—and outraged by anyone who tries to improve it.

Yet there are other poems in which he suggests that his faithfulness to "the ancient way" is more a matter of habit than conviction. In "The Black Cottage," he remembers an old woman who had lost her husband in the Civil War and who used to say (in her "quaint phrase," as Frost calls it) that all men were created free and equal. The old woman was also an orthodox Christian, and her presence in church kept the minister from changing any phrases in the Creed. The minister says, recalling "her old tremulous bonnet in the pew":

> I'm just as glad she made me keep hands off,
> For, dear me, why abandon a belief
> Merely because it ceases to be true.

> Cling to it long enough, and not a doubt
> It will turn true again.

Although the minister is speaking, he seems to express Frost's attitude toward the old New England standards. The poet is more conventional than convinced, more concerned with prudence than with virtue, and very little concerned with sin or suffering; you might say that he is more Puritan, or even prudish, than he is Christian. All the figures in his poems are decently draped; all the love affairs (except in a very late narrative, "The Subverted Flower") are etherealized or intellectualized; and although he sometimes refers to very old adulteries, it is only after they have been wrapped in brown paper and locked away in cupboards. On the other hand, there is little in his work to suggest Christian charity or universal brotherhood under God. He wants us to understand once and for all that he is not his brother's keeper:

> I have none of the tenderer-than-thou
> Collectivistic regimenting love
> With which the modern world is being swept

—and the ancient world was also swept, in the first centuries after Christ. There is one of his narratives, "Two Tramps in Mud Time," that has often been praised for the admirable lesson with which it ends; and yet a professor told me not long ago that his classes always seemed vaguely uncomfortable when they heard it read aloud. It was first published in 1934, and it deals with what seems to have been an incident of the depression years. The poet tells us that he was working in his dooryard on an April day between winter and spring; he was splitting great blocks of straight-grained beech with a lively sense of satisfaction. Two tramps came walking down the muddy road. One of them said, "Hit them hard," and then lingered by the roadside, suggesting wordlessly that he might take the poet's job for pay. The poet assumed that they had spent the winter in a lumber camp, that they were now unemployed and that they had slept "God knows where last night." In life the meeting may have had a different sequel. Perhaps the poet explained to the homeless men that he liked to split his own wood, but that he had other work for them to do; or perhaps he invited them into the kitchen for a slab of home-baked bread spread thick with apple butter. In the poem, however, he lets them walk away without a promise or a penny; and perhaps that explains why a college class—west of the Alleghenies, at least—cannot hear it read without feeling uneasy. Instead of helping these men who wanted to work, Frost turns to the reader with a sound but rather sententious sermon on the ethical value of the chopping block:

But yield who will to their separation,
My object in living is to unite
My avocation and my vocation
As my two eyes make one in sight.
Only where love and need are one,
And the work is play for mortal stakes,
Is the deed ever really done
For heaven and the future's sakes.

The meter and tone of the passage remind us of another narrative poem written in New England almost a hundred years before; but "The Vision of Sir Launfal" had a different moral to point:

Not what we give but what we share,
For the gift without the giver is bare;
Who gives himself with his alms feeds three,
Himself, his hungering neighbor and me.

What Frost sets before us is an ideal, not of charity or brotherhood, but of separateness. "Keep off each other and keep each other off," he tells us in "Build Soil." "We're too unseparate out among each other. . . . Steal away and stay away." In some of his poems he faintly suggests Emerson, and yet he is preaching only half the doctrine of self-reliance, which embraced the community as well as the individual. Emerson said, for example, "He only who is able to stand alone is qualified for society," thus implying that the self-reliant individual was to use his energies for social ends. Frost, on the other hand, makes no distinction between separateness and self-centeredness. In his poems, fine as the best of them are, the social passions of the great New Englanders are diverted into narrower channels. One cannot imagine him thundering against the Fugitive Slave Law, like Emerson; or rising like Thoreau to defend John Brown after the Harpers Ferry raid; or even conducting a quietly persistent campaign against brutality on American ships, as Hawthorne did when he was consul at Liverpool. He is concerned chiefly with himself and his near neighbors, or rather with the Yankees among his neighbors (for although his section of New England is largely inhabited by Poles and French Canadians, there are only two poems in which these foreigners are mentioned). He says when splitting his straight-grained beech blocks:

The blows that a life of self-control
Spares to strike for the common good

> That day, giving a loose to my soul,
> I spent on the unimportant wood;

—and one feels that these blows might symbolize the inward or backward turning of energies in a region that once had wider horizons.

And Frost does not strive toward greater depth to compensate for what he lacks in breadth; he does not strike far inward into the wilderness of human nature. It is true that he often talks about the need for inwardness. He says, for example, in "Build Soil," which for all its limitations of doctrine is the best of his long philosophical poems and perhaps the only one worth preserving:

> We're always too much out or too much in.
> At present from a cosmical dilation
> We're so much out that the odds are against
> Our ever getting inside in again;

—yet still he sets limits on the exploration of himself, as he sets them on almost every other human activity; here again he displays the sense of measure and decorum that puts him in the classical, or rather the neo-classical, tradition. He is always building defenses against the infinite, walls that stand "Between too much and me." In the woods, there is a pile of rocks and an iron stake to mark the limit of his land; and here too:

> One tree, by being deeply wounded,
> Has been impressed as Witness Tree
> And made commit to memory
> My proof of being not unbounded.

The woods play a curious part in Frost's poems; they seem to be his symbol for the uncharted country within ourselves, full of possible beauty, but also full of horror. From the woods at dusk, you might hear the hidden music of the brook, "a slender, tinkling fall"; or you might see wood creatures, a buck and a doe, looking at you over the stone fence that marks the limit of the pasture lot. But you don't cross the fence, except in dreams; and then, instead of brook or deer, you are likely to meet a strange Demon rising "from his wallow to laugh." And so, for fear of the Demon, and also because of your moral obligations, you merely stand at the edge of the woods to listen:

> Far in the pillared dark
> Thrush music went—
> Almost like a call to come in
> To the dark and lament.
>
> But no, I was out for stars:
> I would not come in.
> I meant, not even if asked,
> And I hadn't been.

But Hawthorne before him, timid and thin and conventional as he was in many of his tales, still plucked up his courage and ventured into the inner wilderness; and Conrad Aiken's poems (to mention one example of New England work today) are written almost wholly from within that haunted mid-region. To explore the real horrors of the mind is a long tradition in American letters, one that goes back to our first professional novelist, Charles Brockden Brown. He said in one of his letters, quoted in a footnote by Van Wyck Brooks, "You, you tell me, and one of those who would rather travel into the mind of a plowman than into the interior of Africa. I confess myself of your way of thinking." The same tendency was continued by Poe and Melville and Henry James, and it extends in an almost unbroken line into the late work of Hemingway and Faulkner. But Frost, even in his finest lyrics, is content to stop outside the woods, either in the thrush-haunted dusk or on a snowy evening:

> The woods are lovely, dark and deep.
> But I have promises to keep,
> And miles to go before I sleep,
> And miles to go before I sleep.

If he does not strike far inward neither does he follow the other great American tradition (extending from Whitman through Dos Passos) of standing on a height to observe the panorama of nature and society. Let us say that he is a poet neither of the mountains nor of the woods although he lives among both, but rather of the hill pastures, the intervales, the dooryard in autumn with the leaves swirling, the closed house shaking in the winter storms (and who else has described these scenes more accurately, in more lasting colors?). In the same way, he is not the poet of New England in its great days, or in its late-nineteenth-century decline (except in some of his earlier poems); he is rather a poet who celebrates the diminished but prosperous and self-respecting New England of the tourist home and the antique shop in the abandoned gristmill. And the praise heaped on Frost in recent years is somehow connected in one's mind with the search for ancestors and authentic old furniture. You imagine a saltbox cottage restored to its original lines; outside it a wellsweep preserved for its picturesque quality, even though there is also an electric pump; at the doorway a coach lamp wired and polished; inside the house a set of Hitchcock chairs, a Salem rocker, willow-ware plates and Sandwich glass; and, on the tip-top table, carefully dusted, a first edition of Robert Frost.

NOTES

1. These facts about Hawthorne are taken from F. O. Matthiessen's *American Renaissance [American Renaissance: Art and Expression in the Age of Emerson and Whitman* (New York: Oxford University Press, 1941)], a book that has never been sufficiently praised.—m.c.

Above the Brim

Among major poets of the English language in this century, Robert Frost is the one who takes the most punishment. "Like a chimpanzee" is how one friend of mine remembers him in the flesh, but in the afterlife of the text he has been consigned to a far less amiable sector of the bestiary, among the stoats perhaps, or the weasels. Calculating self-publicist, reprehensible egotist, oppressive parent—theories of the death of the author have failed to lay the ghost of this vigorous old contender who beats along undauntedly at the reader's elbow. His immense popular acclaim during his own lifetime; his apotheosis into an idol mutually acceptable to his own and his country's self-esteem, and greatly inflationary of both; his constantly resourceful acclimatization of himself to this condition, as writer and performer—it all generated a critical resistance and fed a punitive strain which is never far to seek in literary circles anyhow.

Still, it would be wrong to see this poet as the unwitting victim of the fashion which he surfed upon for decades. Demonically intelligent, as acute about his own masquerades as he was about others', Frost obeyed the ancient command to know himself. Like Yeats at the end of "Dialogue of Self and Soul," Frost would be "content to live it all again," and be content also to "cast out remorse." Unlike Yeats, however, he would expect neither a flow of sweetness into his breast nor a flash of beatitude upon the world to ensue from any such bout of self-exculpation. He made no secret of the prejudice

From *Homage to Robert Frost* © 1996 by Seamus Heaney. Reprinted with permission.

and contrariness at the center of his nature, and never shirked the bleakness of that last place in himself. He was well aware of the abrasiveness of many of his convictions and their unpopular implications in the context of New Deal politics, yet for all his archness, he did not hide those convictions or retreat from them.

Frost's appetite for his own independence was fierce and expressed itself in a reiterated belief in his right to limits: his defenses, his fences, and his freedom were all interdependent. Yet he also recognized that his compulsion to shape his own destiny and to proclaim the virtues of self-containment arose from a terror of immense, unlimited, and undefined chaos. This terror gets expressed melodramatically in a poem like "Design," and obliquely in a poem like "Provide, Provide," but it is also there in many of his more casual pronouncements. Here he is, for example, writing to Amy Bonner in June 1937:

> There are no two things as important to us in life and art as being threatened and being saved. What are ideals of form for if we aren't going to be made to fear for them? All our ingenuity is lavished on getting into danger legitimately so that we may be genuinely rescued.

Frost believed, in other words, that individual venture and vision arose as a creative defense against emptiness, and that it was therefore always possible that a relapse into emptiness would be the ultimate destiny of consciousness. If good fences made good neighbors, if (as Ian Hamilton has suggested) a certain callousness of self-assertion was part of the price of adjusting to reality, Frost was ready to pay that price in terms of exclusiveness and isolation, and in terms also of guardedness and irony (and William Pritchard writes well about this in his deliberately positive study of the poet). The main thing is that Frost was prepared to look without self-deception into the crystal of indifference in himself where his moral and artistic improvisations were both prefigured and scrutinized, and in this essay I shall be concerned to show that his specifically poetic achievement is profoundly guaranteed and resilient because it is "genuinely rescued" from negative recognitions, squarely faced, and abidingly registered.

Frost was always ready to hang those negative recognitions in the balance against his more comfortable imaginings. He made it clear, for example, that there was a cold shadow figure behind the warm-blooded image of his generally beloved horseman in "Stopping by Woods on a Snowy Evening":

My little horse must think it queer
To stop without a farmhouse near
Between the woods and frozen lake
The darkest evening of the year.

He gives his harness bells a shake
To ask if there is some mistake.
The only other sound's the sweep
Of easy wind and downy flake.

This rider, faring forward against the drift of more than snow, a faithful, self-directed quester with promises to keep and miles to go before he sleeps, this figure finds his counterpart in "Desert Places," a poem of the same length, written in almost the same rhyme scheme. In "Desert Places" Frost implicitly concedes the arbitrariness of the consolations offered by the earlier poem and deliberately undermines its sureties. The social supports that were vestigially present in "promises to keep" have now been pulled away, and the domestic security of woods with owners in the village is rendered insignificant by a vacuous interstellar immensity:

Snow falling and night falling fast, oh, fast
In a field I looked into going past,
And the ground almost covered smooth in snow,
But a few weeds and stubble showing last.

The woods around it have it—it is theirs.
All animals are smothered in their lairs.
I am too absent-spirited to count;
The loneliness includes me unawares.

And lonely as it is that loneliness
Will be more lonely ere it will be less—
A blanker whiteness of benighted snow
With no expression, nothing to express.

They cannot scare me with their empty spaces
Between stars—on stars where no human race is.
I have it in me so much nearer home
To scare myself with my own desert places.

This poem gives access to the dark side of Frost, which was always there behind the mask of Yankee hominess, a side of him which also became fashionable late in the day, after Lionel Trilling gave it the modernists' blessing in a speech at Frost's eighty-fifth birthday party. Trilling there drew attention to Frost's Sophoclean gift for making the neuter outback of experience scrutable in a way that privileges neither the desolate unknown nor the human desire to shelter from it. I am going to pause with the poem at this early stage, however, not in order to open the vexed question of Frost's dimensions as a philosophical writer or to address the range of his themes or to contextualize his stances, imaginative and civic, within American political and intellectual history. All of these things are worth considering, but I raise them only to salute them dutifully and so pass on to my own particular area of interest.

This arises from a lifetime of pleasure in Frost's poems as events in language, flaunts and vaunts full of projective force and deliquescent backwash, the crestings of a tide that lifts all spirits. Frost may have indeed declared that his whole anxiety was for himself as a performer, but the performance succeeded fully only when it launched itself beyond skill and ego into a run of energy that brimmed up outside the poet's conscious intention and control.

Consider, for example, the conclusion of "Desert Places," which I have just quoted: "I have it in me so much nearer home / To scare myself with my own desert places." However these lines may incline toward patness, whatever risk they run of making the speaker seem to congratulate himself too easily as an initiate of darkness, superior to the deluded common crowd, whatever trace they contain of knowingness that mars other poems by Frost, they still succeed convincingly. They overcome one's incipient misgivings and subsume them into the larger, more impersonal, and undeniable emotional occurrence which the whole poem represents.

I call it an emotional occurrence, yet it is preeminently a rhythmic one, an animation via the ear of the whole nervous apparatus: what Borges called "an almost physical emotion." The tilt of the sound is unmistakable from the beginning. The momentary stay of the stanza is being sifted away from the inside, words are running out from under themselves, and there is no guarantee that form will effect a rescue from danger:

> Snow falling and night falling fast, oh, fast
> In a field I looked into going past . . .

This meter is full of the hurry and slant of driven snow, its unstoppable, anxiety-inducing forward rush, all that whispering turmoil of a blizzard. Here the art of the language is like the art of the French farmer in "The Ax-Helve"; what is said in that poem about the lines and grains of a hickory axe shaft applies equally to the lines of "Desert Places." The French farmer

showed me that the lines of a good helve
Were native to the grain before the knife
Expressed them, and its curves were no false curves
Put on it from without.

The curves and grains of the first two lines of "Desert Places" are correspondingly native to living speech, without any tonal falsity. Who really notices that the letter alliterates five times within thirteen syllables? It is no denigration of Hopkins to say that when such an alliterative cluster happens in his work, the reader is the first to notice it. With Frost, its effect is surely known, like a cold air that steals across a face; but until the lines are deliberately dwelt upon a moment like this, we do not even think of it as an "effect," and the means that produce it remain as unshowy as the grain in the wood:

Snow falling and night falling fast, oh, fast
In a field I looked into going past,
And the ground almost covered smooth in snow,
But a few weeds and stubble showing last.

This feels like an unpremeditated rush of inspiration, and Frost always declared that he liked to take a poem thus, at a single stroke, when the mood was on him. Yet even if the actual composition of "Desert Places" entailed no such speedy, pell-mell onslaught of perceptions, the finished poem does indeed induce that kind of sensation. There is an urgent, toppling pattern to it all, an urgency created by various minimal but significant verbal delicacies—like, for example, the omission of the relative pronoun from the line "In a field I looked into going past." Compare this with "In a field that I looked into going past" and hear how the inclusion of an extra syllable breaks the slippage toward panic in the line as we have it. Or consider how the end-stopping of the first eight lines does not (as we might expect) add composure to them but contributes instead a tensed-up, pent-up movement:

The woods around it have it—it is theirs.
All animals are smothered in their lairs.
I am too absent-spirited to count;
The loneliness includes me unawares.

And where does that line about being "too absent-spirited to count" arrive from? Does it mean that the speaker does not matter? Or something else? In the onwardness of a reading, such curiosity registers fleetingly, like something glimpsed from a carriage window. To count what? The animals? The lairs? And what is "it" that the woods have? Is it snow? Is it loneliness? The speaker is so hypnotized by the snow swirl that he doesn't count as consciousness anymore, he is adrift instead, in the dream of smothered lairs. And those triple masculine rhymes of "fast" / "past" / "last," with their monosyllabic stress repeated again in "theirs" / "lairs" / "awares," are like the slowing of the heartbeat in the withdrawn hibernators.

Halfway through the poem, then, the narcotic aspect of the snowfall is predominant, and the vowel music is like a dulled pulse beat: going, covered smooth, stubble showing, smothered. But in the next eight lines we go through the nature barrier, as it were, into the ether of symbolic knowledge. The consolations of being "too absent-spirited to count" are disallowed and the poem suddenly blinks itself out of reverie into vision. The vowels divest themselves of their comfortable roundness, the rhymes go slender first and then go feminine: "loneliness" / "less" / "express"; "spaces" / "race is" / "places." The repetition which at the start was conducive to trance, and included speaker and reader "unawares," now buzzes everybody and everything awake.

Once again, the effect is not "put on from without," not a flourish of craft, but a feat of technique. There is a disconsolateness in the way the word "lonely" keeps rebounding off its image in the word "loneliness," and the same holds true for the closed-circuit energy of "expression" and "express." Finally, there is a Dantesque starkness about the repetition of the word "stars." Even if these stars are not intended to echo the *stelle* that shine at the end of each of Dante's visions, they still do possess the cold tingle of infinity. So, by such feats of mimesis and orchestration, the speaker's inwardness with all this outward blankness is established long before he declares himself explicitly in the concluding lines. And that is what I meant earlier when I spoke of the excessiveness of the language's own rightness, brimming up beyond the poet's deliberate schemes and performances:

> And lonely as it is that loneliness
> Will he more lonely ere it will be less—
> A blanker whiteness of benighted snow
> With no expression, nothing to express.
>
> They cannot scare me with their empty spaces
> Between stars—on stars where no human race is.
> I have it in me so much nearer home
> To scare myself with my own desert places.

Inevitably, a discussion like this, which concentrates on the poem's musical life, must lead us to take cognizance of Frost's theory of "the sound of sense." This theory, as Frost expressed it in interviews and letters over the years, does fit and complement our experience of what is distinctive about the run of his verse, its posture in the mouth and in the ear, its constant drama of tone and tune. "The sound of sense" presents itself as a technical prescription and serves notice that Frost, even though he broke with the experimental modernists, was still a poet of that critical early-twentieth-century moment, every bit as concerned as the Imagists ever were to heave the art of verse out of its backward drag into nineteenth-century musicality.

A few quotations will suffice to recall the basic convictions which underlay much of Frost's practice; indeed, most of them can be culled from a letter to John T. Bartlett (July 4, 1913), where he begins by distinguishing between the good and bad senses of the word "craft," the bad one applied to those poets whom he calls "mechanics." He goes on then:

> To be perfectly frank with you I am one of the most notable craftsmen of my time . . . I am possibly the only person going who works on any but a worn out theory [principle I had better say] of versification . . . I alone of English writers have consciously set myself to make music out of what I may call the sound of sense. Now it is possible to have sense without the sound of sense (as in much prose that is supposed to pass muster but makes very dull reading) and the sound of sense without sense (as in Alice in Wonderland which makes anything but dull reading). The best place to get the abstract sound of sense is from voices behind a door that cuts off the words . . . It is the abstract vitality of our speech. It is pure sound—pure form. One who concerns himself with it more than the subject is all artist . . . But if one is to be a poet he must learn to get cadences by skillfully breaking the sounds of sense with all their irregularity of accent across the regular beat of the metre.

This gives the main gist of Frost's poetics. It can be supplemented by many other declarations about sentence-sounds and tones of voice, all of which are designed to give an ultimate authority to perfectly pitched natural speech cadences realized in a written text. Such cadences, Frost is at pains to insist, re-establish a connection with the original springs of our human being.

Talking of sentence-sounds, for example, which he elsewhere describes as "the most volatile and at the same time important part of poetry" (the part we can no longer hear in poems in ancient Greek or Latin), he maintains:

No one makes or adds to them. They are always there, living in the cave of the mouth . . . And they are as definitely things as any image of sight. The most creative imagination is only their summoner.

To summon such sounds, therefore, is to recapitulate and refresh a latent resource of our nature: one might say of them what Frost says of the well at the end of his poem "Directive": "Here are your waters and your watering place. Drink and be whole again beyond confusion." And so it follows that a poetry which gives access to origin by thus embodying the lineaments of pristine speech will fulfill, at a level below theme and intention, a definite social function. As Marjorie Sabin has written:

> Frost in 1914 wanted to believe—and wrote poems out of the belief—that human vitality takes on a supra-personal existence in the established intonations of speech . . . What Frost calls "the abstract vitality of our speech" . . . participates in the verbal forms through which other people also enact their lives.

When I fixed upon the title for this essay, I had not read Marjorie Sabin's perceptive comment (included by William Pritchard in *Robert Frost: A Literary Portrait*). But her observation about the vitality of speech taking on a supra-personal existence parallels and answers the things I am hoping to bring into focus through the phrase "above the brim."

This phrase is Frost's own and comes in that heady climbing part of "Birches"—climbing in the musical as much as in the physical sense—where he describes the boy's joyful, expert ascent toward the top of a slender birch tree. Even though the lines that conclude the poem are among some of the most familiar in the canon of twentieth-century verse, I still feel it worthwhile to quote them:

> He always kept his poise
> To the top branches, climbing carefully
> With the same pains you use to fill a cup
> Up to the brim, and even above the brim.
> Then he flung outward, feet first, with a swish,
> Kicking his way down through the air to the ground.
> So was I once myself a swinger of birches.
> And so I dream of going back to be.
> It's when I'm weary of considerations,
> And life is too much like a pathless wood

Where your face burns and tickles with the cobwebs
Broken across it, and one eye is weeping
From a twig's having lashed across it open.
I'd like to get away from earth awhile
And then come back to it and begin over.
May no fate willfully misunderstand me
And half grant what I wish and snatch me away
Not to return. Earth's the right place for love:
I don't know where it's likely to go better.
I'd like to go by climbing a birch tree,
And climb black branches up a snow-white trunk
Toward heaven, till the tree could bear no more,
But dipped its top and set me down again.
That would be good both going and coming back.
One could do worse than be a swinger of birches.

This seesawing between earth and heaven nicely represents the principle of redress which I have elsewhere commended. That general inclination to begin a countermove once things go too far in any given direction is enacted by "Birches" with lovely pliant grace. But my main concern here is with the specifically upward waft of Frost's poems, and the different ways in which he releases the feeling, preeminent in the lines just quoted, of airy vernal daring, an overbrimming of invention and of what he once called "supply." The sensation of lucky strike which he describes in his preface to the *Collected Poems* matches very closely the sensation of flourish and plenty which characterizes "Birches." Here are some relevant lines from "The Figure a Poem Makes":

For me the initial delight is in the surprise of remembering something I didn't know I knew . . . There is a glad recognition of the long lost and the rest follows. Step by step the wonder of unexpected supply keeps growing.

The headiness of Frost's poetry has much to do with this revel in artesian energies, as the poet plays eagerly to the top of his bent and then goes over the top and down the other side. But it is not just the sheer happiness of composition that creates a rise of poetic levels. The opposite condition, the sheer unhappiness of the uncomposed world, is even more conducive to the art of the ascending scale. When Frost comes down hard upon the facts of hurt, he still manages to end up gaining poetic altitude. As his intelligence thrusts down, it creates a reactive force capable of raising and carrying the whole burden of our knowledge and experience.

"Home Burial," for example, is a great poem which ends well above the brim of its last line. Its buoyancy is achieved in direct proportion to its pressure upon the ground of the actual. The poem derives from a cruel moment in the married life of the young Robert and Elinor Frost, when their first child, a boy not quite four, died of *cholera infantum* in 1900; and yet "Home Burial" contains no pathos, no Victorian chiaroscuro. It is one of the best of Frost's dramatic eclogues, with all the rigor and dispatch of Greek tragedy.

A husband comes upon a wife, traumatized by grief at the death of their child, keeping a trembly, furious vigil over the grave. The grave is visible through the window of their semi-isolated house, and is the locus around which their drama of recrimination and rebuke exhausts itself. Indeed, the point I want to make is that the entrapment of the couple, their feral involvement with each other as each other's quarry and companion, is not held at a safe narrative distance but interrupts into the space between reader and text. The mixture of anger, panic, and tyranny in the husband's voice at the end of the poem is rendered with a fairness and bareness that presses closure to an extreme where it virtually constitutes a reopening. The top of the reader's head is lifted like the latch of the protagonist's tormented home, and the lifting power resides in the upsurge of language. Both Randall Jarrell and Joseph Brodsky have written magnificently about the poem in line-by-line commentaries which need not be repeated here. Instead, I will quote the final lines where a premature diminuendo is fiercely contradicted. The husband seeks to clear the emotional air too soon and too proprietorially, in a move to suppress the wildness of the wife's sorrow; but when the sound of *her* sense rises in the perfectly pitched anger, he can no longer restrain the note of tyranny:

> "There, you have said it all and you feel better.
> You won't go now. You're crying. Close the door.
> The heart's gone out of it: why keep it up?
> Amy! There's someone coming down the road!"
>
> "*You*—oh, you think the talk is all. I must go—
> Somewhere out of this house. How can I make
>   you—
>
> "If—you—do!" She was opening the door wider.
> "Where do you mean to go? First tell me that.
> I'll follow and bring you back by force. I *will!*—"

This rising note out of the fallen condition is the essential one which Frost achieves in his greatest work. It is the outcry that comes when he follows his early advice to himself, which was to lean hard upon the facts until they hurt. It is writing which is free of Frost's usual emotional protectiveness, and it represents the highest level of his achievement as a poet.

To say this is not to undervalue the mellow resource of Frost's voice at what we might call cruising altitude, or "middle flight," as Milton called it. In that range, the poet draws *indirectly* upon a wisdom which in his greatest poems seems to be wrested *directly* from experience itself. Yet this indirection of his typical level-best work is not an evasion: within its beguiling melodies there is secluded a strong awareness of that unbeguiling world to which the melodies themselves offer a conscious resistance. Indeed, a recurring theme in Frost's work is the way a particular music can actually constitute a meaning. In "The Oven Bird," for example, the bird has the unique gift of knowing how in singing not to sing; and "The question that he frames in all but words / Is what to make of a diminished thing." On the other hand, the song of the phoebes at the end of the poem "The Need of Being Versed in Country Things" is so perfectly matched to human sentiment that it must be resisted because it is a kind of siren song. The birds come flying through the burnt-out ruin of a deserted house, but even so:

> For them there was really nothing sad.
> But though they rejoiced in the nest they kept,
> One had to be versed in country things
> Not to believe the phoebes wept.

This mixture of the rejoicing notes and the weeping notes, however, is exactly what Frost achieved in the sonnet "Never Again Would Birds' Song Be the Same," which is, among other things, an oblique dramatic statement of his own poetic creed. What we have here is not quite an allegory and not just all orotundity: we have that sensation of speech in free supply, welling up and riding fluently on the old sounds of sense, moving animatedly and skillfully over and back across the pattern of the verse form. Here, too, birdsong, that most conventional of analogies for poetic utterance, is being presented as something bearing traces of prelapsarian freedom and felicity. To misquote Hopkins slightly, it is the note that man was made for. In Frost's trope, the song of the birds is tuned to the note of Eve's voice in Eden, in much the same way as poetry is tuned to the sound of sense, and to those tones of voice that live in the original cave of the mouth. The choral joys of the mythic garden and the actual resource of the vocal cords are harmonized within a wonderful, seemingly effortless heft of language:

> He would declare and could himself believe
> That the birds there in all the garden round
> From having heard the daylong voice of Eve
> Had added to their own an oversound,
> Her tone of meaning but without the words.
> Admittedly an eloquence so soft
> Could only have had an influence on birds
> When call or laughter carried it aloft.
> Be that as may be, she was in their song.
> Moreover her voice upon their voices crossed
> Had now persisted in the woods so long
> That probably it never would be lost.
> Never again would birds' song be the same.
> And to do that to birds was why she came.

"He would declare and could himself believe." The first line is in the conditional, optative mood, so all that follows has to be conditional and in part wishful. There is a lovely certitude in the fantasy, but there is a regretful understanding that it is indeed a fantasy; so there is a counterweight in the line "Never again would birds' song be the same" that works against the poem's logical sense. The poem's argument, as I read it, ought to lead to the conclusion that the changed note of the birds' song should be all occasion of joy, since it happened in Paradise and was effected by the paradisial voice of Eve. But that logic is complicated by the actual note of repining that we hear in the line "Never again would birds' song be the same," a note that comes from the fact that we are now beyond Eden, at a great distance of time and space. The Adam figure, the "he" of the poem, has suffered exile from his prelapsarian bliss, so there is a counterweight of heartbreak in the statement of what seemed in the beginning a heart-lifting truth.

Memories of Eden-like joys corrected and countered by an acknowledgment of their inevitable passing also underlie Frost's poem "To Earthward." This poem takes us back to Frost at his very strongest. It belongs with "Home Burial," but is intensely lyrical rather than starkly dramatic. The quatrains are like fossils, constrained within their shapes but minutely and energetically expressive of the life that gave them shape:

> Love at the lips was touch
> As sweet as I could bear;
> And once that seemed too much;
> I lived on air

That crossed me from sweet things,
The flow of—was it musk
From hidden grapevine springs
Down hill at dusk?

I had the swirl and ache
From sprays of honeysuckle
That when they're gathered shake
Dew on the knuckle.

I craved strong sweets, but those
Seemed strong when I was young;
The petal of the rose
It was that stung.

Now no joy but lacks salt
That is not dashed with pain
And weariness and fault;
I crave the stain

Of tears, the aftermark
Of almost too much love,
The sweet of bitter bark
And burning clove.

When stiff and sore and scarred
I take away my hand
From leaning on it hard
In grass and sand,

The hurt is not enough:
I long for weight and strength
To feel the earth as rough
To all my length.

This poem goes from living and walking on air to living and enduring on earth. It redresses the motion of "Birches," in which the boy climbed in order to be set down. Here the man is sustained even as he seeks to descend. The more he submits himself to the drag of experience and the pull of some moral g-factor, the more a reactive thrust is generated against it. The poetic situation at the end of "To Earthward" is rather different from the pictorial one. Pictorially, we are offered an image of the body hugging the earth, seeking to penetrate to the very *humus* in humility, wishing the ground were a penitential bed. But the paradoxical result of this drive toward abasement is a marvel of levitation: in spite of the physical push to earthward, the psychic direction is skyward. The state of things at the end of the poem is something like that formulated at the end of Frost's sonnet "A Soldier," which deals with the old subject of patriotic death in battle through a beautifully turned conceit. The soldier's body is like a lance in the dust, fallen from its trajectory. Even so, consolation can be found:

> But this we know, the obstacle that checked
> And tripped the body, shot the spirit on
> Further than target ever showed or shone.

The sensation of spirit not so much projected onward as brimming over and above the body is what is thrilling in "To Earthward." There is a wonderful, supple, uningratiating presentation of self going on. the poem does not say "I have faults and deserve to be punished," although it may ruefully admit to this if we put the words in its mouth. Nor does it say "What a good boy am I, to be so grown up at last." Frost is not running for cover behind cocksureness or blandishment, nor is he exercising that verbal sleight of hand which sometimes furnishes too nifty resolutions to other poems. What this poem advances is all guaranteed. It is neither specter nor sculpture: cut this verse and it will bleed. Compare it, for example, with an equivalent poem by Yeats, "Men Improve with the Years," and you are faced with something unexpected: Frost's is the poem in which he walks naked, Yeats's the one which appears more ironical and protected. The warmth of wanting to feel the earth "as rough / To all my length" contrasts well with Yeats's project of coldness in "Men Improve with the Years":

> But I grow old among dreams,
> A weather-worn, marble triton
> Among the streams.

To emphasize this recurring pattern is to highlight something of distinctive and durable value in Frost's work. It does seem to me that the poems which hold up most strongly embody one or the other of the following movements: a movement which consists of or is analogous to a fullness overflowing, or the corollary of that, a kind of reactive wave, a fullness in the process of rebounding off something or somebody else.

For examples of a fullness overflowing without complication, we need to look no further than his first collection, *A Boy's Will*, where the two acknowledged triumphs are "The Tuft of Flowers" and "Mowing." After all, the flowers which are the occasion of the former poem owe their very survival to what Frost calls "sheer morning gladness at the brim," a gladness which inspired the mower to spare them and so, by a little chain reaction of rapture, inspired the poem. Furthermore, in the sonnet about mowing, where the heart of the poetic matter is the whisper of the scythe, that scythe-whisper is itself presented as a welling up of something out of silence, an expression almost of the silence's own abounding relish of itself.

> There was never a sound beside the wood but one,
> And that was my long scythe whispering to the ground.
> What was it it whispered? I knew not well myself;
> Perhaps it was something about the heat of the sun,
> Something, perhaps, about the lack of sound—
> And that was why it whispered and did not speak.
> It was no dream of the gift of idle hours,
> Or easy gold at the hand of fay or elf:
> Anything more than the truth would have seemed too
>   weak
> To the earnest love that laid the swale in rows,
> Not without feeble-pointed spikes of flowers
> (Pale orchises), and scared a bright green snake.
> The fact is the sweetest dream that labor knows.
> My long scythe whispered and left the hay to make.

This early poem broadcasts a sweetness that we credit easily and that we should set in the balance against the tales of the old poet's vanity and vindictiveness. Its melodics possess a wonderful justifying force, and remind us that Frost is, among other things, one of the most irresistible masters of the sonnet in the English language. (Think of the overbrimming technical joys of "The Silken Tent" or the high tides of mutuality in "Meeting and Passing.)

And yet, the bleaker the recognitions being forced upon Frost, the greater the chance of the absolute poem. I am thinking of a work such as "An Old Man's Winter Night," which expresses what I earlier called "the crystal of indifference" at the core of Frost's being, that which takes in and gives back the signals of a universal solitude. Samuel Beckett would surely incline an appreciative ear to the following lines, where the figure of age, in all its factuality and loneliness, is plainly and strangely rendered:

> He stood with barrels round him—at a loss.
> And having scared the cellar under him

> In clomping here, he scared it once again
> In clomping off;—and scared the outer night,
> Which has its sounds, familiar, like the roar
> Of trees and crack of branches, common things,
> But nothing so like beating on a box,
> A light he was to no one but himself
> Where now he sat, concerned with he knew what,
> A quiet light, and then not even that.

To read lines like these is to apprehend fleetingly what Frost means by his compelling if enigmatic declaration in "Mowing" that "The fact is the sweetest dream that labor knows." It certainly would seem that he intends this to be more than a plea for writing as a form of documentary realism. Even though such realism was what Ezra Pound found praiseworthy when he reviewed *North of Boston*—"Mr. Frost's people are real people"—and even though it contributed vividly to my own original pleasure in his work, it is not what the final sweetest dream is about.

In the beginning, however, I did love coming upon the inner evidence of Frost's credentials as a farmer poet. I admired, for example, the way he could describe (in "The Code") how forkfuls of hay were built upon a wagonload for easy unloading later, when they have to be tossed down from underfoot. And sometimes the evidence was more general but still completely credible, such as that fiercely direct account of a child's hand being cut off by a circular saw and the child's sudden simple death. Coming as I did from a world of farmyard stories about men crushed in quarry machinery or pulled into the drums of threshing mills, I recognized the note of grim accuracy in the poem called "Out, Out—." I was immediately susceptible to its documentary weight and did not mistake the wintry report of what happened at the end for the poet's own callousness.

Nevertheless, the counterweight, the oversound, the sweetest dream within the fact—these things are poetically more rewarding than a record, however faithful, of the data. This is why the imagined hardness of "The Most of It" more than holds its own against the cruel reporting of "Out, Out—," why the extravagance of "The Witch of Coös" excels the pastoral of "The Ax-Helve," and why the mysteriously intuited happenings at the end of "Two Look at Two" are more sustaining than the nostalgic wishfulness in the last line of "Directive":

> Two had seen two, whichever side you spoke from.
> "This *must* be all." It was all. Still they stood,
> A great wave from it going over them,

As if the earth in one unlooked-for favor
Had made them certain earth returned their love.

At such moments, and in such poems—if I may repeat my notion one last
time—a fullness rebounds back upon itself, or it rebounds off something or
someone else and thereby creates a wave capable of lifting the burden of our
knowledge and the experience to a new, refreshing plane. Moreover, this
bracing lyric power is as dependent on Frost's sense of his own faults as it is
on his faultless ear. Implicit In many of the poems I have been praising is a
capacity to recognize the shortcomings in himself, and to judge himself for
the shortfall between his life and his art. But what is implicit in the poems is
explicit in a dialogue which Robert Lowell records and which I wish to quote
in conclusion. Here, from Lowell's collection *History*, is part of the sonnet
which he calls plainly "Robert Frost":

> Robert Frost at midnight, the audience gone
> to vapor, the great act laid on the shelf in mothballs,
> his voice is musical and raw—he writes in the flyleaf:
> *For Robert from Robert, his friend in the art.*
> "Sometimes I feel too full of myself," I say.
> And he, misunderstanding, "When I am low,
> I stray away . . ."
>   [. . .]
> And I, "Sometimes I'm so happy I can't stand myself.
> And he, "When I am too full of joy, I think
> how little good my health did anyone near me."

1990

Chronology

1874	Born March 26 in San Francisco, California
1885	Father dies on May 5; Frost, his mother, and his younger sister leave San Francisco to live with his father's parents in Lawrence, Massachusetts
1886	Frost begins working on a part-time basis to support his family
1892	Graduation from Lawrence High School; enters Dartmouth College; leaves Dartmouth before the end of the term and takes a series of jobs in Lawrence
1894	Wanders in the Dismal Swamp between Virginia and North Carolina; returns to Massachusetts determined to prove his worth to Elinor White
1895	Elinor is graduated from St. Lawrence University; she and Frost are married on December 19
1896	Elliott Frost born on September 25
1897	Frost enters Harvard University for the fall term
1899	Drops out of Harvard in April; Lesley Frost born on April 28
1900	Elliott Frost dies on July 8; Frost family moves to farm in Derry, New Hampshire, in October; his mother, Belle, dies
1901	His grandfather dies, leaving Frost the farm and an annuity

1902   Carol Frost born on May 22

1903   Irma Frost born on June 27

1905   Marjorie Frost born on March 29

1907   Elinor Bettina Frost born on June 18 but dies shortly afterward

1912   Frost family leaves for England on August 23

1913   Frost meets Ezra Pound; *A Boy's Will* is published in April; Frost meets Edward Thomas

1914   *North of Boston* is published on May 15; Britain declares war on Germany

1915   Frost family leaves England on February 13; meets Boston literary establishment; begins lecturing and giving readings

1916   *Mountain Interval* published in November

1917   Frost begins teaching at Amherst College during the spring semester; Edward Thomas dies fighting in WW I

1918   Great War ends; Frost contracts severe case of influenza

1920   Frost leaves Amherst College in June; Jeanie Frost committed to the state hospital in Augusta, Maine

1921   Accepts position at University of Michigan in Ann Arbor

1923   Leaves University of Michigan to return to Amherst College; *New Hampshire* published in November

1924   Awarded Pulitzer Prize for Poetry for *New Hampshire*

1925   Returns to University of Michigan for fall semester

1926   Accepts position at Amherst College

1928   Travels with Lillian and Marjorie to France, England, and Ireland; meets with Yeats and Eliot; *West-Running Brook* published

1929   Jeanie Frost dies in mental hospital

1930   *Complete Poems* is published; Pulitzer Prize for Poetry awarded for *Complete Poems;* elected to American Academy of Arts and Letters

1934   Marjorie dies on May 2; Elinor suffers severe heart attack in November

1936	Delivers Charles Eliot Norton lectures at Harvard in March; *A Further Range* published on May 29
1937	Awarded Pulitzer Prize for Poetry for *A Further Range*
1938	Elinor dies on March 20; begins affair with Kay Morrison in the summer
1939	*Collected Poems* is published in January; receives Gold Medal for Poetry from the National Institute of Arts and Letters; accepts position as Ralph Waldo Emerson Fellow at Harvard
1940	Carol commits suicide on October 9
1941	The United States enters World War II
1942	*A Witness Tree* is published on April 23
1943	Frost leaves Harvard to accept a position at Dartmouth; receives unprecedented fourth Pulitzer Prize for Poetry for *A Witness Tree*
1945	*A Masque of Reason* is published; World War II ends; Ezra Pound is confined to St. Elizabeth's Hospital for the criminally insane
1947	*Steeple Bush* is published in May; Frost places his daughter Irma in a mental hospital in August; *A Masque of Mercy* is published in October
1949	Appointed Simpson Lecturer in Literature at Amherst College; *Complete Poems of Robert Frost 1949* is published
1954	Celebrates 80th birthday; travels to Brazil as U.S. representative to the World Congress of Writers
1957	Leaves on May 17 for one-month tour of England and Ireland; receives honorary degrees from Oxford and Cambridge universities in England
1958	Ezra Pound leaves St. Elizabeth's Hospital due largely to Frost's efforts
1961	Reads poem at John F. Kennedy's presidential inauguration on January 20; travels to Israel and Greece in March and April
1962	*In the Clearing* is published; Frost receives Congressional Gold Medal; travels to Soviet Union as part of a cultural exchange in August; hospitalized for prostate cancer
1963	Dies on January 28

Works by Robert Frost

A Boy's Will. 1913
North of Boston. 1914
Mountain Interval. 1916
New Hampshire. 1923
West-Running Brook. 1928
Complete Poems. 1930
A Further Range. 1936
Collected Poems. 1939
A Witness Tree. 1942
A Masque of Reason. 1945
Steeple Bush. 1947
A Masque of Mercy. 1947
Complete Poems of Robert Frost, 1949. 1949
In the Clearing. 1962

Works about Robert Frost

Bagby, George F. "The Promethean Frost." *Twentieth Century Literature* 38.1 (Spring 1992): 1–19.

Barry, Elaine, ed. *Robert Frost on Writing*. New Brunswick, NJ: Rutgers University Press, 1973.

Brodsky, Joseph, Seamus Heaney, and Derek Walcott. *Homage to Robert Frost*. New York: Noonday Press, 1997.

Burnshaw, Stanley. *Robert Frost Himself*. New York: G. Braziller, 1986.

Cowley, Malcolm. "The Case Against Mr. Frost." *The New Republic* (September 11, 1944): 312–313; (September 18, 1944): 345–347. Reprinted in *Robert Frost: A Collection of Critical Essays*. Ed. James M. Cox. (Englewood Cliffs, NJ: Prentice-Hall, 1962): 36–45.

Cramer, Jeffrey S. *Robert Frost Among His Poems: A Literary Companion to the Poet's Own Biographical Contexts and Associations*. Jefferson, NC: McFarland & Company, 1995.

Francis, Lesley Lee. *The Frost Family's Adventure in Poetry: Sheer Morning Gladness at the Brim*. Columbia: University of Missouri Press, 1994.

Frost, Robert. *Selected Prose of Robert Frost*, ed. Hyde Cox and Edward Connery Lathem. New York: Holt, Rinehart and Winston, 1966.

———. *The Poetry of Robert Frost: The Collected Poems, Complete and Unabridged*, ed. Edward Connery Lathem. New York: Owl—Henry Holt and Company, 1979.

————. *The Letters of Robert Frost to Louis Untermeyer.* New York: Holt, Rinehart and Winston, 1963.

————. "I like anything that penetrates the mysteries," in *Interviews with Robert Frost*, ed. Edward C. Lathem. New York: Henry Holt and Co., 1966, 265–266. From a story reported by Thomas Wolfe for *The Washington Post*, May 2, 1961.

————. *Interviews with Robert Frost*, ed. Edward Connery Lathem. New York: Henry Holt and Co., 1966.

————. "The Figure a Poem Makes," in *Robert Frost on Writing*, ed. Elaine Barry. 1939. New Brunswick, NJ: Rutgers UP, 1973, 125–128.

————. "On Emerson," in *Selected Prose of Robert Frost*, eds. Hyde Cox and Edward Connery Lathem. New York: Holt, Rinehart and Winston, 1966, 109–119. "On Emerson" was revised for publication in *Daedalus* in 1959, after originally being delivered as a speech to the American Academy of Arts and Sciences.

————. "The whole thing is performance and prowess and feats of association," in *Interviews with Robert Frost*, ed. Edward C. Lathem. New York: Henry Holt and Co., 1966, 229–236. Extracts from an Interview of Frost by Richard Poirier. Originally appeared in Number 24 (Summer/Fall 1960) issue of *The Paris Review.*

————. "The Prerequisities," in *Robert Frost on Writing*, ed. Elaine Barry. New Brunswick, NJ: Rutgers University Press, 1973, 137–139. Previously published in the *New York Times Book Review*, March 21, 1954 and as the preface to Frost's *Aforesaid*, 1954.

————. "To *The Amherst Student*," in Barry, Elaine, ed. *Robert Frost on Writing*. New Brunswick, NJ: Rutgers University Press, 1973, 112–114. Reprinted from *The Amherst Student*, March 25, 1935.

————. "To F.S. Flint," in *Robert Frost on Writing*, ed. Elaine Barry. New Brunswick, NJ: Rutgers University Press, 1973, 82–84.

————. "To Kimball Flaccus," in *Robert Frost on Writing*, ed. Elaine Barry. New Brunswick, NJ: Rutgers University Press, 1973, 111–112.

————. "To Lewis N. Chase," in *Robert Frost on Writing*, ed. Elaine Barry. New Brunswick, NJ: Rutgers University Press, 1973, 69–71.

————. "To Sidney Cox," in *Robert Frost on Writing*, ed. Elaine Barry. New Brunswick, NJ: Rutgers University Press, 1973, 66–69.

Gould, Jean. *Robert Frost: The Aim Was Song.* New York: Dodd, Mead, 1964.

Heaney, Seamus. "Above the Brim." in *Homage to Robert Frost* by Joseph Brodsky, Seamus Heaney, and Derek Walcott. (New York: Noonday Press, 1997): 57–88.

Holland, Norman N. *The Brain of Robert Frost: A Cognitive Approach to Literature*. NY: Routledge, 1988.

Kearns, Katherine. *Robert Frost and a Poetics of Appetite*. NY: Cambridge University Press, 1994.

Lentricchia, Frank. *Robert Frost: Modern Poetics and the Landscapes of Self*. Durham, NC: Duke University Press, 1975.

Liebman, Sheldon W. "Robert Frost, Romantic." *Twentieth Century Literature* 42.4 (Winter 1996): 417–437.

Lowell, Amy. *Tendencies in Modern American Poetry*. New York: Macmillan, 1917.

Lowell, Robert. "Robert Frost: 1874–1963." *Selections: From the First Two Issues of* The New York.

Review of Books, eds. Robert B. Silvers and Barbara Epstein. (NY: The New York Review of Books, n.d. [reprint]): 75–78.

Maxson, H.A. *On the Sonnets of Robert Frost: A Critical Examination of the 37 Poems*. Jefferson, NC: McFarland & Company, 1997.

Meyers, Jeffrey. *Robert Frost: A Biography*. New York: Houghton Mifflin, 1996.

Monteiro, George. *Robert Frost and the New England Renaissance*. Lexington, KY: University Press of Kentucky, 1988.

Mulder, William. "Freedom and Form: Robert Frost's Double Discipline." *South Atlantic Quarterly* LIV (July 1955): 386–393.

Murray, Keat. "Robert Frost's Portrait of a Modern Mind: The Archetypal Resonance of 'Acquainted with the Night.'" *The Midwest Quarterly* 41.4 (Summer 2000): 370–384.

Newdick, Robert S. "Robert Frost and the Sound of Sense." *American Literature* IX (November 1937): 289–300.

Nitchie, George W. *Human Values in the Poetry of Robert Frost: A Study of a Poet's Convictions*. Durham, NC: Duke University Press, 1960.

O'Donnell, William G. "Talking about Poems with Robert Frost." *The Massachusetts Review* 39.2 (Summer 1998): 225–249.

Oster, Judith. *Toward Robert Frost: The Reader and the Poet*. Athens: University of Georgia Press, 1991.

Parini, Jay. *Robert Frost: A Life*. New York: Henry Holt, 1999.

Richardson, Mark *The Ordeal of Robert Frost: The Poet and His Poetics*. Urbana: University of Illinois Press, 1997.

Saltzman, Arthur M. "Futility and Robert Frost." *The Midwest Quarterly* 41.3 (Spring 2000): 289–301.

Sergeant, Elizabeth Shepley. *Robert Frost: The Trial by Existence.* New York: Holt, Rinehart and Winston, 1960.

Stambuk, Andrew. "Learning to Hover: Robert Frost, Robert Francis, and the Poetry of Detached Engagement." *Twentieth Century Literature* 45.4 (Winter 1999): 534–552.

Thompson, Lawrance. *Robert Frost: The Years of Triumph, 1915–1938.* New York: Holt, Rinehart and Winston, 1970.

———. *Robert Frost: The Early Years, 1874–1915.* New York: Holt, Rinehart and Winston, 1966.

———. *Fire and Ice: The Art and Thought of Robert Frost.* New York: Russell & Russell, 1942.

Thompson, Lawrance, and R. H. Winnick. *Robert Frost: The Later Years, 1938–1963.* New York: Holt, Rinehart and Winston, 1976.

Wakefield, Richard. "Thomas Eakins and Robert Frost: To Be a Natural Man in a Man-Made World." *The Midwest Quarterly* 41.4 (Summer 2000): 354–369.

Walsh, John Evangelist. *Into My Own: The English Years of Robert Frost.* New York: Grove Press, 1988.

Whicher, Stephen E., ed. *Selections from Ralph Waldo Emerson: An Organic Anthology.* Boston: Riverside, 1960.

Wilde, Oscar. "The Decay of Lying." (from *Intentions*) *The Artist as Critic: Critical Writings of Oscar.*

Wilde, ed. Richard Ellmann. Chicago: University of Chicago Press, 1982: 290–320.

Wilson, Edmund. "The All-Star Literary Vaudeville." *The Shores of Light: A Literary Chronicle of the Twenties and Thirties.* New York: Farrar, Straus, & Young, 1952.

Winters, Yvor. "Robert Frost, or The Spiritual Drifter as Poet." *Sewanee Review* LVI (1948): 564–596. Reprinted in *Robert Frost: A Collection of Critical Essays,* ed. James M. Cox. Englewood Cliffs, NJ: Prentice-Hall, 1962.

WEBSITES

The Academy of American Poets – Robert Frost
http://www.poets.org/academy/news/rfros

Amherst Common
www.amherstcommon.com/walking_tour/frost.html

The Friends of Robert Frost
www.frostfriends.org/

Modern American Poetry – Robert Frost
www.english.uiuc.edu/maps/poets/a_f/frost/frost.htm

Perspectives in American Literature – Robert Frost
www.esustan.edu/english/reuben/pal/chap7/frost.html

The Robert Frost Web Site
www.robertfrost.org/

Contributors

HAROLD BLOOM is Sterling Professor of the Humanities at Yale University and Henry W. and Albert A. Berg Professor of English at the New York University Graduate School. He is the author of over 20 books, including *Shelly's Mythmaking* (1959), *The Visionary Company* (1961), *Blake's Apocalypse* (1963), *Yeats* (1970), *A Map of Misreading* (1975), *Kabbalah and Criticism* (1975), *Agon: Toward a Theory of Revisionism* (1982), *The American Religion* (1992), *The Western Canon* (1994), and *Omens of Millennium: The Gnosis of Angels, Dreams, and Resurrection* (1996). *The Anxiety of Influence* (1973) sets forth Professor Bloom's provocative theory of the literary relationships between the great writers and their predecessors. His most recent books include *Shakespeare: The Invention of the Human*, a 1998 National Book Award finalist, and *How to Read and Why*, which was published in 2000. In 1999, Professor Bloom received the prestigious American Academy of Arts and Letters Gold Medal for Criticism.

BRUCE AND BECKY DUROST FISH are freelance writers and editors who have worked on more than 100 books for children and young adults. They have degrees in history and literature and live in the high desert of Central Oregon.

THOMAS MARCH received his M.A. and Ph.D. in English and American Literature from New York University. His primary research interests are 20th-century British and American literature, with special emphasis on the novel, psychoanalytic theory, and the representation of consciousness. He has published numerous essays on the works of 20th-century British and American writers, including George Orwell, E.M. Forster, Virginia Woolf, Anais Nin, Edmund Wilson, Saki, and Bessie Head. His short fiction and poetry have appeared in *Anais*, *Atenea*, *Verbatim*, and *The Yalobusha Review*.

MALCOLM COWLEY (1898–1989) was an American literary historian and scholar whose productivity and prominence extended from the Paris of Hemingway and Fitzgerald through the 1980s. He published several volumes of literary criticism, including *Exile's Return* (1934), *A Second Flowering: Works and Days of the Lost Generation* (1973), and *A Many-Windowed House: Collected Essays on American Writers and American Writing* (1970), among many others. He was a member of the American Academy of Arts and Letters, of which he served as chancellor from 1967–77. Cowley was instrumental in the publication of Viking's *Portable Faulkner* in addition to anthologies of such other American literary greats as Hemingway, Emerson, and Whitman.

Irish poet SEAMUS HEANEY received the Nobel Prize for Literature in 1995. He has published numerous volumes of poetry, including *Death of a Naturalist* (1966), *Wintering Out* (1972), *Station Island* (1984), and *Seeing Things* (1991).

Index

10/02

811
Frost
Robert Frost

GAYLORD S